Contents

SECTION ONE

In Pursuit of a Successful, Top-Dollar Exit

N⊘B.S.

GUIDE TO

SELLING

YOUR COMPANY FOR

TOP DOLLAR

THE ULTIMATE NO HOLDS BARRED PLAN TO BUILDING A 7-FIGURE OR 8-FIGURE BUSINESS AND MAXIMUM WEALTH

Dan S. Kennedy and David Melrose

Ep
Entrepreneur
PRESS®

Entrepreneur Press, Publisher
Cover Design: Andrew Welyczko
Production and Composition: Alan Barnett Design

Library of Congress Cataloging-in-Publication Data

Names: Kennedy, Dan S., author. I Melrose, David (Entrepreneur), author.
Title: No B.S. guide to selling your company for top dollar / by Dan S.
   Kennedy with David Melrose.
Other titles: No bullshit guide to selling your company for top dollar
Description: [Irvine] : [Entrepreneur Press], [2025] I Series: No B.S. I
   "With guest interviews with Brian and Adi Kaskavalciyan, Dr. David
   Phelps, Stan Kinder, Jonathon Cronstedt, Ted Oakley"—Title page. I
   Summary: "Your No B.S. guide to building and growing your business to
   make a successful, top dollar exit"— Provided by publisher.
Identifiers: LCCN 2024010642 (print) I LCCN 2024010643 (ebook) I ISBN
   9781642011715 (paperback) I ISBN 9781613084830 (epub)
Subjects: LCSH: Sale of business enterprises. I Sale of small businesses.
Classification: LCC HD1393.25 .K46 2025 (print) I LCC HD1393.25 (ebook) I
   DDC 658.1/64--dc23/eng/20240426
LC record available at https://lccn.loc.gov/2024010642
LC ebook record available at https://lccn.loc.gov/2024010643

SECTION TWO

Interviews with Company Owners about Their Exits

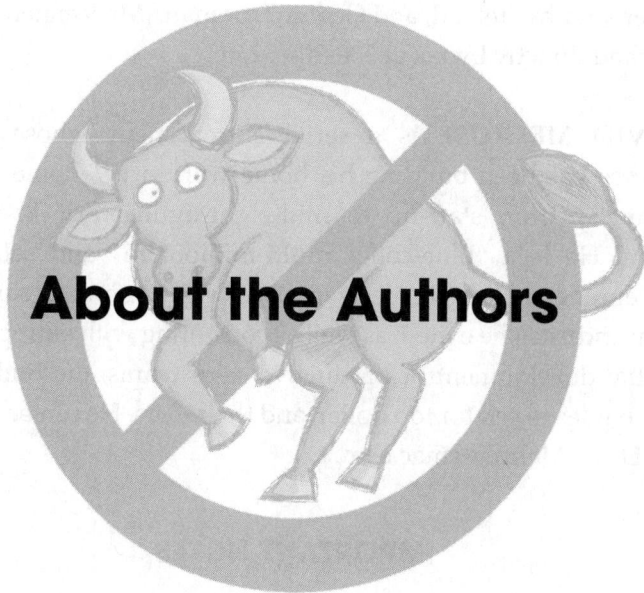

About the Authors

DAN S. KENNEDY is a from-scratch multi-millionaire serial entrepreneur who has started, built, bought and sold companies, been a founding investor in a hugely successful software company, and has helped many business owners build diverse businesses to seven-, eight-, and even nine-figure valuations and exits. The company he founded and continues working with that serves entrepreneurs worldwide can be seen at MagneticMarketing. com. Mr. Kennedy is also the author of the NO B.S. series of books and other books available at Amazon, and is a sought-after strategy consultant, direct-response copywriter, and business coach. As a speaker, he has repeatedly shared the stage with former U.S. presidents, champion professional and Olympic athletes, Hollywood celebrities, and celebrity entrepreneurs as well as Zig Ziglar, Brian Tracy, Tom Hopkins, and Jim Rohn. His own conferences have featured Gene Simmons (KISS), Joan Rivers, Kathy Ireland, and George Foreman. Mr. Kennedy can be reached directly by fax at 330-908-0250.

DAVID MELROSE is a serial entrepreneur whose biggest success has been building his home warranty / home services company from start-up to mid-eight-figures exit in just 4.5 years. He is a "blue-collar multi-millionaire" and self-taught entrepreneur. He is currently involved with a new start-up in the same industry he exited, as well as consulting with entrepreneurs on the development of productive sales teams, the building of companies to sell for top dollar, and their exits. He can be reached via DavidMelrose@mac.com.

IMPORTANT NOTES

It is impossible to avoid talking about legal matters with the subject of selling your company, but no one contributing to this book is an attorney. We are NOT dispensing legal advice, nor should any of our comments be taken as a substitute for advice you may need from a licensed legal professional. Here, we are sharing our experiences and opinions and describing what we have done personally. Any decisions you may make that you attribute to any comments here on legal issues is still your sole responsibility. Neither the authors, contributing guests in interviews, the publisher, or related parties accept ANY liability for your decisions or actions.

IN PURSUIT
OF A SUCCESSFUL,
TOP-DOLLAR EXIT

Important Author's Introduction NOT to Be Skipped

by Dan Kennedy

Dorothy, We're Not in Kansas Anymore!

You have built a successful business, so you are smart, capable, tough, and very likely to be a DIY'er and a "control freak." Welcome to the club. Good news: Some—but only some—of what you've thought, done, and used to create your success to this point is fully relevant to the entirely "new business" you are beginning: the sale of your company. But bad news: Some of what got you to this dance won't be helpful at all and can even get in your way in this new venture, the selling of your company. I urge you to think of this as a "new business," and being humble enough, or at least ego-checked enough, to acknowledge that succeeding in this will require *different* thinking and actions than what you have previously relied on. Your obtaining this book suggests that understanding. Good.

In this book, I have shared my experiences, my co-author David Melrose has shared his, and I have assembled five sellers of companies, all students or clients of mine, who have generously shared their experiences. This is like a guided tour of Oz, after you've arrived from Kansas. You'll see that the logic of conducting business back home is not the logic, or often illogic, of selling your company in Oz. You are a stranger in a strange place, inhabited by some pretty strange critters, like Private Equity Investors, who do NOT look at a business as you do; Venture Capitalists; Idiot Bankers; and Bloody, Sword-Wielding Deal Killers. By the time we've taken this guided walk down the yellow brick road and you finish this book, I promise you will see the sale of your company differently than you imagine now. And you will be better empowered to navigate Oz on your own, going forward.

This is *not* an exhaustive textbook on the sale of a business, full of EBITDA, accrual vs. cash accounting, balance sheets, and other CPA and banker stuff. You can get all that elsewhere, easily. (Your present CPA might not be the right resource; I recommend finding one with experience with clients selling their businesses.) Instead, this book is a collection of personal experiences in building companies, readying them to sell, and selling them—*for above-par prices, on seller-friendly terms*. Further, it is a sales and marketing book, not a finance book. We have approached the sale of our own businesses (and clients' businesses) as a marketing and selling project. Positioning, packaging, and presenting the business as a "product" and as an opportunity. Searching for, finding, or attracting the right buyer. Asking for and getting a higher price than normal, customary, ordinary valuation formulas would provide. This is vital, because this may be the last money you get. You are turning off the water faucets at their source and leaving with a garage full of full water bottles. Full, but they do not magically refill themselves. Few sellers fully grasp the ramifications of this. Post-sale, they are later surprised by their new reality.

When I was on a celebrity-loaded speaking tour for nine years, at big arenas in 25+ cities a year, I got to know Barbara Bush backstage. She told the story of the morning after exiting the White House, home in Texas, waking to find George sitting up in bed, staring off into space—stunned to the point of paralysis because nobody had brought coffee and the morning newspaper. He had been president, before that VP, before that CIA director, and it had been a long time since nobody was there to bring him things. I hear from sellers of companies all the time about their surprises after their exits, including the same kind of one experienced by George Bush. No secretary. No assistant. And, gee, no paycheck. One of the best responses to all this is: money. So, it is important to sell for top dollar. This book is meant to facilitate that.

One of our goals is to reduce your surprises about selling and about life after selling.

In these pages, you'll find real-world stuff. Not academic classroom information. Everything here is experience based, not theoretical, not regurgitated from predecessor books. In short, it is "NO B.S." You will discover, for example, that any standard formula for valuation should be ignored. The value of a business is different to one buyer vs. another. The right buyer can overpay yet get a bargain, an ideal situation for a seller. When Bob Iger bought Marvel for Disney, the business media was full of criticism for his gross overpaying for what Marvel was worth. But the critics did not understand what Bob did, about what Marvel could *uniquely* be worth *to Disney*. There are all sorts of reasons different buyers buy different businesses—reasons that defy or transcend or at least mitigate the limits of standard valuation. This is just one gold key to selling at top dollar. You're about to delve into this one and many more.

I am quite proud of the number of small business entrepreneurs who started "with me," in my No B.S. world with start-ups or very small, very ordinary businesses, and creatively built large, extraordinary businesses sold for tens of millions, hundreds of millions of dollars, even in one case, a billion dollars. David Melrose's mid-eight-figure sale is one of many. An enormous amount of wealth has been created. Being in business often only creates income, with lifestyle unwisely allowed to elevate in tandem with rising income, and it is damnably hard in our regressive, punitive tax system to siphon off wealth from your income. It can and should be done, but rarely is. Most business owners have wealth captive inside their companies, thus only "on paper" and "in theory," until they sell. I sincerely want you to be wealthy.

So, my friend, welcome to Oz. Let's start looking around...

CHAPTER 1

I Started, I Built, I Sold— and You Can, Too

by David Melrose

This is my story, as background for the advice I have for you in this book. I've been an entrepreneur since the early 2000s. I got into my first business the same way I got into my last—the one I sold for the mid-eight figures—by seeing someone else having success and realizing, if they can do it, surely I could, too. This an important difference between true entrepreneurs and just about everybody else. When ordinary people see somebody doing something they think of as extraordinary, they do not immediately think that they could do it, too, if they wanted to. Instead, they think of the reasons why they can't. The entrepreneur sees the same thing and automatically credits himself with the ability to use the example as a start-point or as a whole example he can use if he chooses.

Long ago, I realized that good ideas are a dime a dozen. Getting off your ass and executing is where the money is. Almost any business will do. People tell you to follow your passion, do something you enjoy, and the money will follow. It's better to find industries and businesses with good cash flow, a reasonable barrier to entry, and if you want to sell, buyers in the market. Yet, my first statement stands: Almost any business will do. Almost any business can be made valuable and saleable.

I grew up poor, dirt poor, like no running water or flushable toilets poor. Single mom, who worked two jobs, I skipped a lot of school and flunked out of college. No silver spoons here. But no complaints. Mom (God rest her soul) gave us everything we needed. Although it may have come from Goodwill or secondhand, it was good enough.

I screwed around a lot when I was younger, chasing women, drinking beer, waiting tables, and I even had a failed Hollywood acting career. Just having a good time. In my late 20s I started realizing that L.A. sucks, and really sucks if you aren't rich and famous. Time for a change.

I loaded up my 1980s Bronco with everything I owned. I'd bought the vehicle at a "Buy Here Pay Here" place in Torrance, using a fax machine as a down payment. Driving an old car for the first time through the California desert on the way to Texas wasn't the smartest choice I've ever made. My hands white knuckled the steering wheel as the temperature gauge rose steadily from F, to O, to R, and stopped just short of D (Ford). Sunset mercifully came and the needle fell, crisis averted. As night came, I needed to sleep. I didn't have enough money for a hotel, so I found a well-lit parking lot, parked on a hill in case the car wouldn't start, and slept in the front seat. Morning came and I turned the key to start the car—of course the battery was dead. Luckily I rolled down the hill, the Bronco lurched as I pop started it using the clutch, and the engine roared to life. Off to my friend's house.

While I pondered my life choices as I prayed to make it the last few hundred miles, I realized I was tired of being broke and it was time to grow up and make some money.

In the distance, I could see my friend's place, and while I am not particularly religious, I did thank God. The final turn lay ahead; the truck died as I rolled down the road. I popped the clutch—nothing. God has a sense of humor. The Bronco coasted the last hundred yards, left turn, another left, and into a parking space. Barely made it, blew the timing chain.

Broke and unemployed, I did what I did best—drank beer and chased girls. It was a great summer. As summer ended, I made a friend who had a sales job at a retail mortgage call center and was making bank. Great, get me a job. As I came up to speed in my new sales job and the industry, it was becoming obvious that there was a lot of money in mortgages and not a lot of bright people. I fit right in.

After working for a year in a cubicle, Lady Luck smiled. I got fired. Fortunately, I found a new job selling mortgages to brokers, "wholesale" rather than "retail." Meeting with brokers, I represented a variety of mortgage products and saw a whole new world. These guys were printing money! $5,000, maybe $10,000 in commissions for one loan. Insane.

Maybe you can guess what I was thinking: *If they could do it...I could, too.* Of course, it's not *that* easy. Or *that* simple. But I want you to understand that I was not a sophisticated man. I was a rough-around-the-edges, crude, chronic goof-off trying to turn a corner in my life and be an entrepreneur—and get rich. You are probably much better qualified for your run to building and selling your company for seven figures or mid-eight figures or more. Having now spent a lot of time around many successful entrepreneurs, I think that the entrepreneur at heart has a somewhat arrogant mind. My mind just assumed I could do this. I gathered some friends, got licensed, and we hung out our shingle. We were off to the races. Not knowing much, we just acted "as if" and B.S.'ed our way through the process, learning along the way. About this time, I discovered Dan Kennedy. While I had sales experience, marketing and business were new concepts to me and I knew if we were going to survive we better learn those parts of having a real business, and fast. I spent two years attending marketing conferences, joining mastermind groups, reading, and listening to everything Dan had. This led me from being just about making money to owning a business that could make money, for me and for others. I've come to appreciate the distinction. A lot of small businesses let the owners make money, but aren't organized to be scalable or saleable.

Dan once mentioned that little hinges swing big doors and you never know when someone will say that one thing that makes hopping on a plane, staying in a hotel, and sitting in a cold meeting room for two days pay off like a slot machine. He admitted it was self-serving, but true nonetheless. Still, I hated conferences. Not my thing. But I went, to try and speed the rate at which I went from "simple" to sophisticated about business success.

How We Built to Be Saleable

We used a lot of "Danisms" in our business. They paid off. Dan once said, "Ain't no amount of money made or no amount of money saved that is worth one night in jail with Bubba as your bunk mate." I heeded his warning. We kept on the straight and narrow. Never took a shortcut, never committed fraud on a loan. We might have been the only mortgage broker in the country who didn't. No kidding and no exaggeration. Years later, after the crash, the FBI knocked on the door of a guy I knew, took him to jail for loans he did fraudulently five years earlier. Never wanted any part of that. Thanks, Dan.

It's probably a good time to preach a little about ethics and karma. Karma exists. It might be slow, but it's real. Maybe not in the exact way the Hindus say, but bet your bottom dollar, if you are breaking the laws or regulations, or for that matter, just being a piece of crap in general, the train is coming and will run you over one day. It's much more profitable to do the right thing, avoid the short-term gain to avoid the long-term pain. Like Chris Rock says, "A moment of pleasure can be a lifetime of pain." Shortcuts are tempting at the beginning, when you are struggling just to meet payroll. Shortcuts are tempting later when you are trying to accelerate growth. Shortcuts are tempting toward exit, when you are trying to make your company match up with buyers' preformed desires. Shortcuts will always loop back around to bite you. If you are ever going to sell a company and walk away safe, it has to be "clean" from top to bottom all along or at least cleaned up before taken to market. No skeletons in closets.

How I Got from "There" to Sell

One business led to another, some failed, others worked. The winners paid for the losers many times over. The business I sold was born out of a loser. Silver linings can be true. In fact, my loose research says that over 80 percent of the companies that sold for eight figures and higher, or taken public, started out as something much different than they evolved into. The big examples are Disney, Amazon, and Apple. Well over half of all multi-millionaire entrepreneurs have at least one miserable failure in their history. In many cases, it birthed their successful business. This is true, incidentally, of Dan Kennedy. He took over a severely troubled, small, but publicly traded company, failed to turn it around, ultimately had it go into bankruptcy, but spun out of it the new company that would evolve and be built into the hugely successful company he sold. Brian Kaskavalciyan, interviewed later in this book, came right out of failure in business to start the one that made him rich by exit. You may or may not need to modify and evolve your current business into something that is "the same but different" as you move toward a top-dollar sale. If you do, that's fine.

Over time we got better, and smarter. Trial and error paid off, aggressively getting information paid off, hard work paid off, and the money rolled in. Personally, I didn't really care about the money very much. At heart, I am a loafer and I had small kids and wanted to spend time with them. For me, the business gave me freedom to do whatever I wanted.

After a few years, I was clearing seven figures while working about 5 to 10 hours a week. With the exception of the occasional emergency that was all hands on deck until the problem was solved, life was good. Free time was spent training Brazilian Jiu-Jitsu, working out, spending time with the family and on personal development and education. Strong mind, strong body. This went on for nearly two decades. This is what business ownership is supposed to do for you. It is what a business *has to be* doing for you to be saleable at top dollar. It has to be fully functional without you starting it up every morning and being with it every day.

In 2015, we decided to dabble in an automotive services company. What a loser. Lost a small fortune. The thing went belly-up within a year. Luckily, in its death throes a representative of a vendor happened to come in to shoot the breeze and casually mentioned a home services product that they hadn't been able to make work for over a decade and asked if we wanted to give it a shot. We didn't know it at the time, but that meeting was about to make me very rich. Every skill, every advertising, marketing, and selling method that I had learned and developed for the successful mortgage business was perfectly transferable to this "thing."

There are, by the way, a ton of perfectly marketable and saleable products lying around in the hands of people with no idea what to do with them or how to sell them.

We started the home services business immediately, moved what we knew from our other business over to it, and figured out the rest on the fly. Revenue grew slowly at first but then boomed, and profits followed. All the years of learning about building the right culture, sales and marketing systems, employee training, and compliance paid off. The home warranty / home services industry was the ideal place for me and my team.

I Set Out to Sell the Company

As a business owner, I always considered it a goal to build and sell a company one day. It may be the pinnacle of an entrepreneur's career. It includes recognition of your worth and of what you are able to create and develop, from an objective outside source. It definitely gets the respect of people around you. It may also be the only opportunity to get rich from your small company. You might never be able to take enough money out of it as you operate it, after taxes, to turn into wealth, but with its sale comes a multiple. Three, five, eight, ten times your business's gross or gross profit or net, paid all at once. My exit payday was mid-eight figures, making financial security for my family and freedom for me possible. I knew all this, and with this company thriving and growing by formula, system, and its team, I started thinking seriously about its sale. For the first time, I had something that *was* saleable.

This is something you have to recognize: Is your company saleable? If not, why not? Then fix it so it is.

The Reality of Selling Your Company

Selling is a real pain in the ass. It's a lot of work. A LOT. At the end, the buyer is going to try to nail you, one way or the other. A favorite trick is last-minute renegotiation after due diligence.

Jonathan Cronstedt talks about this in his interview in Chapter 15. I got a lot of advice during the sale, most of it: "Be happy with the money you get up front—you'll likely never see another penny without a lawsuit." Turned out to be true. That is not always the case. Dan, and the Kaskavalciyans (Chapter 12), both have happy tales to tell about post-sale outcomes. But if you play the odds, you'd bet on the buyer finding a way to avoid paying you the earliest discussed price, the LOI price, and to avoid paying you post-sale money. There is a lot of romance, love, and enthusiasm until the time comes for a check to actually be written.

Dan often tells the story, meant as a parable, of the actor James Garner dying without ever seeing a penny of residual money from his popular TV series *The Rockford Files*. At one point he was told the problem was with his contract because "Jim, in Hollywood, there ain't no net." He also tells Burt Reynolds' story about the executives at Pontiac being so thrilled with the huge popularity and sales boost of their Trans-Am caused by the Smokey and the Bandit movies that they promised Burt a new car every year for life. After a few years, the cars stopped coming. He waited two years before complaining and Burt was then told, "That promise was from the *former* vice president. *He's* dead now."

I saw a lot of this "creativity" coming from the acquirer of my company, before, during, and after the sale.

There was a lot of number crunching, late nights, and stress. Fortunately for me, my staff did most of the work. Selling is also an emotional roller coaster. Most of my employees were great and I had a lot of affinity for them, and not working together was going to hurt. Business gave me purpose and was fun. I had mixed feelings about my decision as the sale moved forward. You probably will, too. Ultimately, I decided to take my chips off the table. I'd never have to work for money for the rest of my life (assuming I didn't blow it, hat tip to Ted Oakley; see Chapter 16), and I'd have to run the business for much longer to get the same amount of cash, and that meant no blowups, politically, economically, or competitively during that time. That's a lot to ask. Selling was de-risking in a big way.

If I wanted to, I knew I could do it all again in three years, post-non-compete, and I had that tucked in the back of my mind. There's a James Bond movie titled, *Never Say Never Again.*

Initially they offered me numbers I couldn't refuse. A lot of it in stock, a lot of it in earn-outs. The numbers were so big that those two things didn't matter much to me. Due diligence took a year. I sold to a publicly traded company and they had some big guns working the deal and they went through everything with a fine-tooth comb. The big day came and *they slashed their offer by two-thirds!* They based the offer on a multiple of earnings, which they discounted for a number of B.S. reasons, a few days before closing. OK, no problem. I was on the fence anyway. The cash was pouring in, I liked what I was doing, and we were growing. They were "real sorry," but they could only pay me a fraction of the initial offer. "It was out of their hands," you know; "they had a board to report to." Well, I had a board to report to as well, and my wife agreed they could go impolite-verb themselves.

Apparently, they needed me a little more than I needed them. They kept negotiating with themselves and upping their offer. I changed mine to all cash, all up front. No stock, no earn-out. Ultimately, they did it my way minus a small holdback. It literally happened at the last minute and the team of attorneys on both sides worked overtime to meet prior deadlines. It felt like a high-stakes poker game. Who was bluffing?

Was it worth it? 100 percent. I would do it again. Too much risk not to. Too many unknowns. Strategically taking chips off the table is a necessary part of gaining wealth. Selling a business is a big leap.

Timing matters. Selling in advance of some substantial change in the market, or your business can be the difference between being rich or poor. Check out how Mark Cuban got so rich. And how the buyer of his company ate the losses. I think you sell when you can, for a reasonable payout, because once you've done it once, you can do it again.

That is one of the next chapters in my story, occurring as I write this: the formation of a new company in the same businesses as the one I sold, which I intend to build faster and smarter, to be even more valuable. I'm also doing a little consulting with entrepreneurs preparing their companies to sell. I took 2 years off. I'm ready.

CHAPTER 2

My Story of Selling My Company

by Dan Kennedy

I sold my first business, a small ad agency and commercial art studio, in 1978, in order to move from Ohio to Arizona. We were coming out of record-breaking winters, in cold and in snow. My #1 client had closed up shop, and moved there. I woke up in a hurry. In hindsight, I don't think I would have done much better on the sale had I been more knowledgeable and patient. The business was not worth a great deal, and the buyer was wealthy and indulging her bucket list item, so she overpaid. Frankly, I got lucky. Fortunately, I knew it, so I made a point of educating myself about selling businesses before the next opportunity to do so occurred. Again fortuitously, I picked up the biggest mid-level M&A and business brokerage firm at the time as a consulting client, and I learned a lot by hanging around them and understanding how they repositioned, repackaged, and prepared a business to take to market.

I sold the next company I built from scratch for millions in 2004. Then I participated in its sale four more times via what I call "equity without equity."

It's important to understand that future, not yet existent money is easier to get than present, existing money. By getting future money, you can effectively inflate the total price you are getting for your company and even share in unpredictable upside. I'll use my personal experience as the example, then further explain the strategy.

In order for my own example to make sense to you, as I reference it throughout this book, I'm going to have to briefly describe it. It's not a simple, normal business like a group of restaurants or shoe stores. My company, originally "Kennedy Inner Circle," sometimes "No B.S. Inner Circle," then "GKIC" (for: Glazer-Kennedy Inner Circle), served small business owners with a collection of information products like monthly newsletters and courses, seminars and conferences, tele-coaching, mastermind groups, and vetted vendors. The relationship with its customers was structured as "membership," with automatically charged monthly dues, at three different price and benefit levels. This gave the business multiple income streams, but as base it had recurring revenue, a very attractive feature to many buyers of companies. The current version of this, No B.S. Inner Circle/Magnetic Marketing, can be seen at MagneticMarketing.com, and there is a Free Gift Offer from it on page 153. It is owned by ClickFunnels, a large marketing software company. In between my creating it and now, it was sold *five* times. The important request I'll make is that you not get too distracted by the exact nature of my company and think my experiences with it do not apply to yours. That would be a mistake. The strategies drawn from or used in my experiences can easily translate and apply to any business and its sale.

Now, let me quickly explain "equity without equity." While selling 100 percent of my company, as part of that agreement and the 3-year post-sale, defined roles work-for-hire agreement, I obtained royalties tied to certain upsides, such as the number of active recurring revenue members, but maybe most importantly, to the sale price of that buyer's next sale. The bad news of such an arrangement is that the royalties are taxed as earned income, not capital gains. The good news is that, as a non-owner, I had *zero* liability for anything, and *zero* managerial responsibilities. There could be no partner-type arguing over decisions affecting net profits because I did not own any of the company; I received royalties on gross results. Fly first class, fly coach, hire circus performers for the next event, or don't; I can be emotionally distanced and practically disinterested. This arrangement is unusual. Unheard of, by many business brokers, lawyers, CPAs, and sellers. That does *not* make it impossible to get. Just unusual and unheard of. I have not only secured lucrative equity without equity when selling my company, and even when that buyer sold, with the new buyer; I've also gotten it with a few consulting contracts.

If you have particular expertise or are, in any way, extraordinarily desirable to retain in some role(s) with the business and you are of arguably greater value than just the very common 3-year-after-sale available if needed for advice and some post-sale communication with customers, then you have the basis to obtain the same kind of unusual contract and compensation that I did.

If you prefer actual equity, maybe in a case where the future more likely holds an IPO than another sale, you can get that instead of equity without equity. Just remember that you never get what you don't ask for.

Normal. Customary. Standard Terms.

Way back when, Hollywood operated on a studio system. Actors, actresses, movie stars were all under multi-picture, multi-year contracts, typically salary based, with little or no bonuses tied to a film's success. At one point, actors with enough popularity balked. The whole system collapsed and was rebuilt, favoring the stars. They became freelancers, they got negotiated fees per picture, and they got "points." Way back, TV stars got no royalties. Then that changed. We can go industry by industry. Until somebody asked, nothing changed—it was just the way it was done. Somebody who the studio, the network, etc. really, really, really wanted suddenly made a whole new kind of compensation structure demand—and got it. Such secrets are hard to keep. You really can't just cede and surrender to usual, normal, and customary. You can define your worth, persuade others of your worth, and get your worth.

With the first sale of my company, I got about what it was worth in cash, but I got a collection of back-end and upside royalties that proved 10X more valuable than the cash sale price. This was not a surprise to me. I knew I was betting on a good horse. A capable entrepreneur, marketer, and small company CEO, willing to do certain things the company needed for growth that I, by personal preferences, would not do. I could, but I wouldn't. We were also at the nascent stages of online marketing and online publishing, very likely to multiply the business' size and speed of growth. You have to try to see into your crystal ball about the future of the company you are selling, in the hands of the people you are selling it to, when going down this equity without equity, upside path, or if taking actual equity.

This money is only imaginary money that does not yet exist, so it is easier for the buyer to agree to than it is for the buyer to part with more cash now or to take on more debt via seller financing.

Whatever you decide to include in your deal, keep in mind it may be the last such deal of your life. Even if it isn't, it will at the very least be the one that makes the next one possible. Common advice is to leave no money on the table, and that's fine, but I'll add—leave no share in upsides on the table that might have been gotten either.

CHAPTER 3

Who Buys Small Businesses and Mid-Sized Companies?

by Dan Kennedy

You can sell Upstream, Downstream, Sideways, Internally, and "Odd."

Selling Upstream

Selling Upstream usually involves a business like yours, even a competitor, or a synergistic business, bigger than yours. There can be varying motives for their purchase. That's important. A number of different possible motives, not just growth by acquisition.

I once sold the manufacturing portion of a company I had in a difficult turnaround situation to a bigger, direct competitor, but the purchase was not made based on my business's value at all. My production equipment was old and essentially obsolete. The business was losing money, in part due to a ridiculous level of debt service laid on it by its prior operators, but in part because the costs of production with the obsolete equipment and buying raw materials in small quantities left little margin. But I was still a tough, capable competitor, in fact, a better marketer. We both did business in a relatively small niche, exhibited across the aisle at the same trade shows, mailed to the same list, dealt with the same prospects and customers. My superior selling capability and fierceness at this forced my competitor to spend an inordinate amount of money on his marketing that, if I were gone, could literally stop. I pitched buying my company to him based on *that*. Projected savings in dollars from less need of aggressive marketing, plus projected income from clients collected by their being orphaned (at better margins than mine) × 5 years, plus added value of more formidable size thus barrier to new, upstart competition equals greater value of his company, plus no more headaches and ulcers from combat with me…equals asking price of "XXX." In this case, it was the assumption of a certain amount of debt (which *he* could easily refinance on better terms) plus a cash payment roughly equivalent to what I might squeeze from continuing as is over the next 3 years. This freed up resources to grow the remaining, more profitable portion of the business (not directly competitive with his—in fact, it became his customer). He made a try at negotiating, but surrendered quickly to my asking price and terms. Deal was done in 48 hours. In essence, he bought the business as a means of paying me to go away.

As the old joke goes, I've been thrown out of better places than that, but never paid to leave.

Once, a major brand name soft drink company* bought a small, local chain of pizza shops in Michigan* for a price at least triple what that business was worth by any normal valuation. Why? They wanted to market test having such shops sell only one brand's beverages, which was not then being done. If this seems like a question that might have been answered in a simpler, less costly manner, you're right. But they wanted to do it "in the dark," with as few people knowing about it as possible. The seller and the employees retained all signed NDAs (non-disclosure agreements). The seller was made quite rich. Then a surprise— not only did same-store sales not suffer from the switch to only their brand's beverages, but they discovered they could do well in the very profitable pizza business. The result is a large beverage company, today, owning a major pizza brand and chain. (I have withheld names out of necessity.)

I did a lot of consulting with WeightWatchers® after they had been acquired by Heinz®. It was an odd acquisition. Heinz® bought it to get the brand for frozen food products to be sold in supermarkets, a distribution channel they dominated. They would have been much better advised to just do a licensing deal, but they bought the entire company because they could—with a very poor understanding of what made it tick. They did a fair amount of damage to it and later sold it. Similarly, I did a lot of consulting with Miracle Ear®. That founder sold, bought back, sold, bought back, and sold that company. Big companies routinely buy, screw up, and sell back small companies they buy. If you want to know why this happens, read the excellent book *The Founder's Mentality*.

Today, PE, Private Equity, is in the mix, with small to mid-sized businesses—generally speaking, defined by having 500 to 5,000 employees. According to *Shark Tank*'s Kevin O'Leary, that bracket of businesses provides 62 percent of the jobs. PE looks at it principally as an opportunity for profit by financial engineering, not necessarily its own growth or success. This means the PE buyer believes they can improve your company's profitability and/or resale value by reducing expenses and better operations management, by reallocated ad spend and better marketing, or by merger or synergistic connection to other businesses they own. If PE buys two retail office supply store chains, they intend to close some stores close to each other and put both customer populations into the one remaining, thus cutting lease, employee, and other overhead costs without reducing revenue and by cutting executive overhead—each company has a CEO, CFO, COO, accounting team, etc., and both combined as one entity needs only one each. PE typically looks for situations it can go into and exit in 3 to 7 years. Sometimes they take intended gains in advance by placing debt on the acquired company(ies). PE also usually takes deal-making and management fees, paid to itself. This whole process was once focused only on large businesses, but it has now moved down into the mid-sized range. One of my businesses was sold to a PE group, an experience I recount elsewhere in this book.

There are also PE-backed consolidators vacuuming up small, independent businesses in a number of categories including dental practices, optometrist practices, veterinary practices, funeral homes, retirement / assisted living facilities, and others. In these cases, there is an operator focused both on financial engineering and on growth, with its chief financing from PE. A good example as of this writing is Heartland in dentistry. A lot of this comes to you; you don't have to hunt for it. They often exhibit at industry trade shows and conferences, have agents in the field calling on business owners, and otherwise aggressively hunting for "ripe" acquisitions. Sometimes strong-arm tactics are used, such as the threat of "if we don't buy you, we will buy one of your competitors, fund them richly, and put you out of business. It's like three crooks with the DA on a TV cop show; only one gets a deal; the first in wins." Of course, this comes with their "standard formula" for valuing your business and their "normal and customary" terms.

Consider a client's dental practice. He had built an exceptionally successful, exceptionally profitable "boutique" practice specializing in whole mouth restoration and cosmetic cases. The practice was thriving and impressive when a PE-backed corporate operator of hundreds of practices came to call. Their other practices were more bread 'n butter, ordinary, "fix it, doc, it's broke" practices, so the corporate buyer drooled all over themselves at my friend's practice's numbers. His sky-high fees, big case sizes, and high profit margins all made them want to get into his type of practice, although, privately, they thought him a fool for his high new patient acquisition costs caused by the exceptional advertising and marketing system he had built with my assistance. They were sure they could improve on his numbers by cutting a lot of those costs as well as by replacing overpaid staff members. They kept this to themselves as they wooed him. Not only was he offered an attractive pile of money, although calculated by their standard formula for buying all practices, with no premium for how "premium" his was, but they promised him an enduring love affair post-sale. He would stay involved for 5 years, be their "chief strategy advisor," continue as "the face" of the practice to be very slowly and gently phased out over years. Come in to do dentistry only with the most complex cases. For this, a monthly consulting fee and a bonus percentage on growth. There was even a chance he'd get a marketing consulting and training gig with the company as a whole. And, totally flexible hours, so he could finally take the cruises and trips his wife had been demanding for years. Wowza. He was hurried along from first date to marriage, by the enthusiasm *for him* expressed by the buyer and by a threat that if they couldn't come to terms easily, they'd move on to a competitor in the area. He signed a lot of "standard and customary" clauses in a lot of documents. He did exit with a hefty price to brag about, but a goodly portion was tied to contingencies he never collected.

Immediately, and I mean *immediately*, after the sale, a horror show began. A corporate transition team descended. The system of generating new patient leads from a mix of online and offline advertising with offers of free books and information kits, sending out hardbound books and media packages, follow-up by Federal Express, was all stopped. The ads were switched to pitching appointments and exams. Some of the media was moved online, some eliminated altogether. Long-tenured, highly capable but high paid staff were let go and replaced with young, fresh-out-of-school, much cheaper people (poorly matched with the patient demographics). He was sidelined. Called in if needed. Managed by a boss half his age. Virtually everything about his practice was scalped. By the 6th month, he was so miserable, he negotiated an early exit, sacrificing a considerable amount of money that, in his mind, and his retirement financial calculations, he had as his. He found himself bound up and chained by a collection of NDA, non-compete, percentage reduction of sale price installments, and other "uglies" he had paid no heed to, as they were "just standard and customary"; just "boilerplate," and he didn't think they'd ever apply to him. He didn't miss out on growth bonuses though; a year later the practice was half the size it was when the corporate giant acquired it. Two years later, they sold it to a young dentist, fresh out of school, for a fraction of what they paid for it.

This is a surprisingly common story. You *can* sell Upstream to people who don't understand your business, sometimes for a fine payout, but there's often a price paid for doing so, after the sale, if you have any back-end financial arrangements, or if you care about what happens to the business.

Yet another Upstream potential buyer can be a vendor of yours. Often, a manufacturer or supplier is generating small, tight margins while watching your company sell what they have made at big margins. Your pasture looks a lot greener than theirs. If you have your business highly systemized, which we talk about in my interview with Jonathan Cronstedt (Chapter 15), your vendor can spread his wings and take over your business, then be his own best customer for his original business. If you are the vendor, a similar scenario can occur, with your best customer buying you in order to add your profit margin to theirs and have more control over their supply chain.

You should never rule out selling Upstream, despite cautions and horror stories. It's too big and likely a potential buyer pool to snub your nose at. In these instances, an all-cash exit is best so you have none of your purchase price tied up in contingency-governed payouts. If that's not possible, then every single caution in this book about deal structure, reasonable expectations for post-sale, etc., is of prime importance.

Selling Downstream

I sold my main company, which I built from scratch, Downstream. The perfect candidate buyer was present, as a customer/member of it and a private client of mine.

This same company was sold Upstream some 10 years later, to an entrepreneur in partnership with a PE group. That ran its course very much like the dental practice example I recounted earlier in this chapter. The PE group, its investors and point-person, and the entrepreneur did due diligence on all the math, which appeared very appealing, but they never understood the true nature of the company's business or what made it produce its attractive numbers. Even I was shocked at how little curiosity they showed. The fellow I had sold to, who made this sale, made a bad post-sale deal, was surprised at the way changes were made, grew miserable and angry, and essentially paid to exit early. I had made a much better post-sale arrangement and, despite watching them make a bloody mess of things, I kept up my end of the deal, stayed around in agreed-upon roles, and got paid. When he abruptly exited, they came to me for help; would I step back in to do X, Y, and Z? I then got to renegotiate and put in place a new, lucrative contract of my making and writing. When their inevitable sale, just getting out with skin and tail 'tween their legs, occurred, I was still paid on the sale (for my equity-without-equity provisions—see Chapter 2), and I obtained a whole new contract of my making with that new buyer. I even got a six-figure signing bonus like a pro athlete. Note: If you don't ask, you'll never know what you could have gotten.

Anyway, back to selling Downstream. You may find good candidates with a business like yours but smaller or versions of yours in constrictive niches who will buy you to leap up, rather than slowly climb up. To purchase speed. To purchase status or prestige. To leapfrog over a bigger competitor. The fact that they are smaller does *not* mean the owners do not have or cannot get or borrow the capital necessary for the purchase. You should never rule out a prospective buyer based on your assumptions about their financial position.

Sometimes you can sell Downstream to an employee or group of employees. There are certain structures for this like an ESOP, territory for knowledgeable CPAs and tax attorneys. Often, there is a key employee or a group of employees capable of taking over, and interested in doing so, especially versus the alternative of a new owner who's a stranger, putting their job security at risk. Or the business being closed. The usual obstacle is: money. Whether or not the employee(s) will have or can borrow or can raise the funds you require will be a roadblock. One way to circumvent it is if the company itself, with its own credit (free of your personal guarantees), can borrow, use the borrowed funds to pay you, and have the new owners take over that debt. Another is for the key employee, owner-to-be to assemble a group of investors. Another is for you to offer owner financing and be the bank. While every seller prefers 100 percent of the sale price in cash, at sale, for good reasons, roughly two-thirds of deals do not happen this way. In two-thirds of small company sales, the seller is holding a note for some portion of the sale price and/or accepting some after-sale, back-end money or upside in trade for a reduction in the cash required at the time of sale. This puts you at significant risk of having to repossess and rescue a damaged, mismanaged business or of not getting fully paid, period. You have to weigh those risks against the other options, if any, you have for the sale, the relative difficulty of other options vs. ease of the seller-financed deal, the time lost to continuing a search for a different future buyer, your confidence in the buyer's capabilities, and more. It's rarely a simple decision. It shouldn't be colored by friendship or family relationship. The correct question is: Would I do this deal if John weren't a longtime friend or a blood relative?

Keep in mind, there is only one way a seller-financed deal can work out perfectly for the seller, but there are dozens of ways it can go awry. Some can be mitigated. You might, for example, insist on being the beneficiary of a life insurance policy covering the debt until it is paid off, that policy paid for by the buyer. That takes care of the risk of him being hit by a bus. In some cases, you can sell a transferable note to private note buyers / investors at a significant discount, and if you got a high enough sale price that the discounted amount from the note buyer is satisfactory, you can cash out, no more worries. If you have a worthy potential buyer stopped only by insufficient cash, you *can* definitely get creative.

Yet another Downstream buyer can be a vendor of yours, who can expand vertically by buying you. I once worked with a fantastic entrepreneur who had built a great specialty book and newsletter publishing business. It started very small. It grew and grew over about two decades. His main vendor, a printing company, grew right along with him. At the start, they were a little two-man retail print shop, doing his jobs at night. Then they had to buy additional equipment, get more space, hire more people. All nicely profitable, but all very dependent on the entrepreneur's publishing business. For health reasons, he rather suddenly decided to retire, and he had no sons or daughters or other family to take over the business. He was wealthy enough to just quit. He was not interested in going through a long, protracted search for a buyer. He laid all this out for me, and I said, "*Force* your printer to buy your company. Finance some of it if you must—you don't actually need this money, you can set up a monthly income, and if somehow you wind up not collecting it all, so what?" I also told him to make the promissory note personally secured by the individual and to make it transferable. His pitch was: Buy this or I'm just going to shut it down. The print shop owner had actually been quietly envying the much higher profits the publishing entrepreneur made on each book than he did doing all the heavy lifting of making them, warehousing them, and shipping them. He *wanted* that business. A deal was made in a matter of days to everybody's satisfaction. The printer paid $500,000 of a $2 million sale up front in cash, the balance over 72 months at 6 percent annual interest. The business could easily handle that payment, essentially paying itself off, leaving the printer with it free and clear going forward after the 72 months. It was arguably free to buy and paid for itself, he had to buy it, he secretly wanted to have it, and my friend got exactly what he wanted. Also, by carefully writing a narrow, tight non-compete agreement, he was able to offer himself as a consultant to other newsletter publishers and enjoyed several such arrangements, consulting from his new beachfront home in the Florida Keys.

Selling Sideways

This might involve a direct, comparably sized competitor or extremely synergistic business.

A synergistic deal example is Aspen Dental and ClearChoice. One of the biggest general dentistry chains and one of the biggest implant dentistry chains. Either one might have bought the other. Each had patients ready-made for the other.

Companies can only grow three ways:

1. Building
2. Inheriting
3. Buying

A company can manufacture its growth by taking market share from competitors or by diversifying to sell more to its customers, through its own creative invention, innovation, superior advertising, marketing, or selling. A lot of companies built this way initially get less and less able to do it the bigger they get. They are like that gigantic dinosaur with the disproportionately short arms and tiny paws. Big, but not very capable. Organic growth takes time, patience, persistence, ingenuity—and capital. It's not free.

A company can grow by inheriting the orphaned customers of a dead competitor. Borders bookstores' death sent a lot of orphaned customers to Barnes & Noble. This happens in our economy, locally, regionally, and nationally, from time to time. When Bed Bath & Beyond closed all its stores, it didn't have enough customers to support itself (and its monstrous debt), but it *did* have a lot of loyal customers. They scattered, to Kohl's, to HomeGoods, online to Amazon. BB&B returned, reinvented, as e-commerce only, its fate yet unknown. But an alert, proactive chain could have mounted a big effort to invite these orphaned customers in.

A company can grow by acquisition. This has many attractions. It's faster than building, it requires less ingenuity than building, it can be a lot easier to finance than building, and it can take a competitor off the map. You can make your company an attractive acquisition to a horizontal competitor by these features: leapfrogging and speed of growth for them, income and cash flow and redundant expenses to be reengineered to pay for the financing of the acquisition, and the elimination of a pesky competitor to boot. What's not to like about all that?

CHAPTER 4

**Built to Sell
MARKETING**

by David Melrose

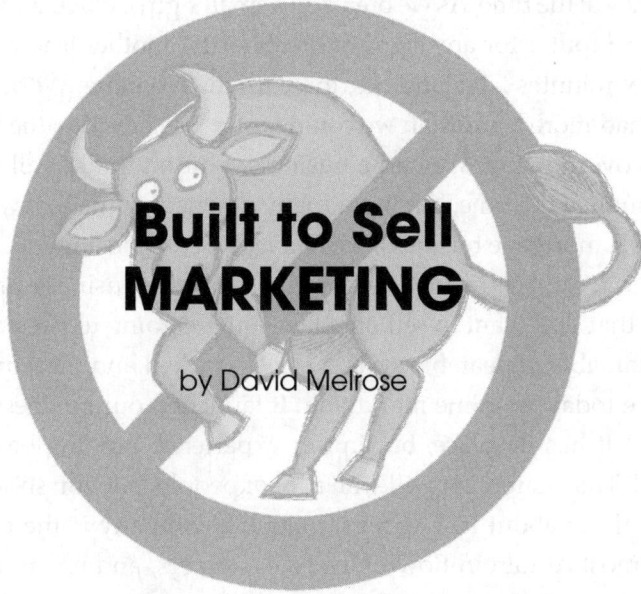

W hen we started in business in early 2000, we knew
absolutely zero about marketing. Pay per clicks and
Internet marketing were in their infancy and we dove
in headfirst. Competition was scarce and ROI was pretty good.
With a small investment in a website and $2,000 to our name, we
utilized every pay per click site available at the time. Hundreds
of keywords for pennies per click. In our small office we held our
breath as we hit the "Go Live" button on all of our campaigns. It
basically came down to this. It will work and we are in business
or it'll flop, my last $2,000 would be gone, and I'd be searching for
a job. Wife was thrilled, as you'd imagine.

About an hour had passed as we sat in the borrowed desks
and chairs when we got a notification of a lead. One is better than
nothing. Since I was the best salesperson of the group, it was on me

to work the lead. Called him up, he answered, and the sale went smooth. We stood to make $5,000 on that loan, which was a ton of money at the time. As we breathed a small sigh of relief, we watched the computer for any signs of life. Shortly, another lead comes in; a few minutes later, another; three more, five more. Within hours, we had more leads than we could work. The next day the mailbox was overflowing. We had a business. I didn't think it all the way through at the time, but it gradually dawned on me that we didn't have a mortgage business; we had a *marketing* business.

You can't count on a lucky strike to build a business, much less one that you want to sell one day. You are going to need a stable, sustainable, repeatable system that is tracked and measured. The craze today is online marketing. It launched our business at that time. It has its place, but in our experience nothing beat direct mail. That statement will stun a lot of people, but you should stop and think about it. The most valuable company is the one with the most certain in-flow of leads, customers, and revenue. Every online media is fragile. The most stable media is mail. The USPS is a huge employer, a quasi-government employer that is too big to be allowed to fail. No algorithm inspects your mail and what you say in it and how you say it. As soon as we tested mail and made it work, I knew it had to be *a foundation* for our business.

Marketing is something you are going to have to learn; it is the most valuable part of the business. Great at customer service? Great, get a job. Great salesperson? Awesome, go sell cars. Marketing makes it all happen. Without it, you don't have a business. The math is simple—can I get a paying customer for a fraction of the amount he is paying me? If so, you can multiply that.

Scientific Marketing Creates Value

Split testing a new piece or form of marketing against your control (what works now) is something you need to master. You have to test everything as you never know what small change can make a big difference. It could be the envelope, the copy, the list, whatever—there are lots of variables. The important thing is you are constantly testing new ideas against your control piece (the one bringing in all the money). Which brings us to tracking. Stats are the lifeblood of your company. In marketing, it's how much mail, how many calls, what is the close rate, revenue per sale, cancellations, lifetime customer value, etc. Too many business owners have no clue what their numbers are. I had to learn all this. You can, too. A good place to start are the books *No B.S. DIRECT Marketing for NON-Direct Marketing Businesses, 4th Edition* and *No B.S. Guide to RUTHLESS Management of People and Profits, 2nd Edition.*

You will build a more profitable business with direct-response-type, scientific marketing, and you'll have a much better story to tell when it comes time to sell.

Being Marketing Oriented, VERY Marketing Oriented

Earlier in the book we talked about how little hinges swing big doors, and you never know when someone will say that one thing that makes the light bulb go off. It happened to me many times, but one memorable occasion was at one of the Kennedy Super Conferences I attended. Dan took the stage and said that your marketing pieces in any media should have every type of contact for your business on it (email, phone, fax, etc.) and there should be no empty space on your entire piece. Upon returning to the office, I pulled out our control piece and pondered what Dan said. The back of the letter was empty. Aha! To the chagrin of my employees and against the advice of the naysayers, I put a full mortgage application on the back of our letter and our fax number. Out goes the mail, the fax machine starts humming. Hundreds of applications pour in. Call volume does not decrease. *Jackpot.*

It is these kinds of discoveries that can give you a competitive edge, better ROI on advertising, faster growth, even faster growth to being ready to sell. The only way you get them is by observing, listening, and experimenting. Testing, endlessly.

Of course, the sales reps didn't want the fax leads and wouldn't work them (we will address this later), so I had my wife and a couple telemarketers take them. Sales take off. The sales reps then complain they don't get the "special" fax leads. This makes me happy, and an extra million dollars a year.

We played with lots of tests over the years. We mailed phones, voice recorders, and all types of trinkets. But ultimately what it comes down to is this—you have to have a repeatable model that is trackable and scalable. It also needs to have some complexity to discourage competition copycats (to the greatest extent possible). A dependable media, an effective message, a repeatable model, a system, all accurately tracked is Built to Sell Marketing.

For those of us not born with rich parents, or not lucky enough to get an Ivy League education and the connections that come with it, or who are not destined to start the next Tesla, the way to wealth for the common man is to be an expert marketer. While other skills are needed, this skill is the most important, the most lucrative, and surprisingly not that difficult to learn. Study, test, and repeat. Constantly.

Resource Box

The Special Gift offer on Page 153 is your new passkey to the whole world of scientific, organized marketing.

CHAPTER 5

Built to Sell SALES

by David Melrose

My mom worked mostly secretarial-type jobs and the odd part-time restaurant job to help make ends meet. Occasionally she would take on some additional work in sales: cable TV sales, water filtration sales. We would sit in the kitchen and she would practice her sales pitches on me. It was interesting to hear her. She had some success. But with two small kids, a commission-only full-time sales job was never in the cards. Still, it gave me the idea that if something better doesn't come along, maybe I could always sell something. Being a single mom with two boys wasn't easy, but she made it work. While we weren't the best behaved kids, my brother and I didn't cause our mother too much grief. Growing up, I had no idea what I wanted to do, but after (barely) graduating high school my friends and I worked at Olive Garden. It was my first sales job.

After many years of waiting tables (and having a blast) I got a little burned out on the industry and was looking for a change. Sales seemed like the next best thing. Job searching in Los Angeles was a bit of a challenge due to the size. Traffic, even back in the '90s, was terrible. My first Sunday evening in Los Angeles I sat in my room listening to the radio. It was midnight and the DJ came on with a traffic update. Incredible. The place is unlivable now. If you know, you know. One day, while searching the job ads in the paper, I saw something very familiar. "Cable sales rep wanted!" Wow, perfect. I had no experience, but I was familiar with the industry and rode out with my mom on sales calls a few times. My interview was with Jim Brown, an older, well-dressed black man, who always wore nice suits. I was able to B.S. my way through the interview and was hired. He was a fantastic boss.

Walking door-to-door selling cable subscriptions was fun! West L.A. has a ton of interesting people and I must have knocked on 10,000 doors that first year. I've been run off by gang bangers, challenged (and lost to) Dr. Dre in a Madden NFL game, got my only acting role, and came to be known as the "cable guy" by a number of Hispanic girls who all attended the same high school. But most importantly, it gave me a foundation in sales. That foundation includes a positive attitude about it—while most people carry negative attitudes—and an understanding of its importance.

One of the famous sales trainers, David Sandler, founder of Sandler Selling Systems®, says: If you don't have a system for selling, people default to their systems for not buying. Partly thanks to Dan Kennedy, I've studied Sandler, Tom Hopkins, Zig Ziglar, and others. They are all devout believers in planned and scripted presentations, a set pathway for the sales conversation to follow. I built all this into my company, and not only did it drive our success, it demonstrated to my acquirer that we were not a ragtag bunch of cold-call cowboys.

If marketing is the king of business, sales is the queen. Once you break the marketing code, sales is not a tough nut to crack. Selling is easy—putting together a strong sales team isn't. Culture matters. If you aren't careful in your hiring or you have a bad culture, you will have a merry band of scallywags that would make Blackbeard blush. They might get sales, but at some serious costs, like buyer's remorse, cancellations, and reputational damage.

Most salespeople are a product of their environment, and many companies have a make-money-at-any-cost model. Damn the customer. Not a formula for long-term success. Those companies do the bare minimum, push the gray areas, and hope for the best. Some industries are more prone to it than others. Be careful of ever chasing a leader of a pack that doesn't care about stability or company equity. Be very wary of employing salespeople or sales managers who aren't concerned with those things either.

It's a problem we've had in more than one company. It takes a little prodding, but most come around. The ones that don't are quickly fired. However, we are big on what Reagan said to Yeltsin, "Trust but verify." We believe you are doing what you are told, but we are going to double-check it anyway. Sometimes the little devil on the shoulder tempts them. Compliance is there to give them that extra incentive to do the right thing. I've taught my team that we need high sales productivity, but a certain kind of it; not any kind of it, at any cost.

Nothing Left to Chance

To build a valuable company, you need a system of selling, a good training program, the right people, and an aligned compensation system. If your compensation plan is not well thought out and aligned with the company's goals, you can bet your bottom dollar the sale reps will find a way to game it. It is a constant battle of cat and mouse. Even if you have a good culture and hired the right people, your sales team will figure out every loophole within weeks. Guaranteed.

A good sales system should:

- Be simple. The simpler, the better.
- Have incentives that spur efforts—but not lying or cheating.
- Have good selling scripts.
- Have predetermined, proper answers to questions and objections.
- Have a way to "tag team" leads.
- Have a follow-up system, including calls for: no appointments, appointment, no sale, and any other misfire.
- Have a method, if possible, for immediate upsells or cross-sells for happy new customers.
- Include multi-media, multi-step follow-up (rarely left just to salespeople).
- Have a compliance process, to ensure that the company's policies are being followed.
- Incorporate constant measurement and accountability.

If you are missing any of these, or are weaker in some than others, roll up your sleeves and go to work.

Dan once told us a story of little Charlie. Charlie's mom came to Charlie and said, "Charlie, I am going to the store. Do not eat any of the cookies out of the cookie jar—it will spoil your dinner." Well, Charlie is watching and if Charlie doesn't see Mom check the cookie jar when she comes home, guess what happens next time she goes to the store? Same thing with your sales reps. You can talk till you are blue in the face, but if you need or want something to be said or not said to your customers, you better be listening.

Sales Management by (Realistic) Objectives

You have to decide on what Dan calls "Good Enough Numbers." Always strive to beat them, but also be realistic about them. You are not going to make every sale; you are not going to get every lead worked properly. Good Enough will make you a lot of money. Good Enough is better than most companies will ever do, and Good Enough will make your business sellable. We spent tens of thousands on consultants, read tons of books, beat ourselves to death trying for perfection, and at the end of the day it never moved the needle more than Good Enough. The quicker you learn this lesson, the easier your life will be. Don't get me wrong, there is value in continuing education, but when you get to Good Enough, time to move on to Next. There are often good opportunities in a business neglected by being too obsessed and occupied with trying for perfection with things where 80 percent is Good Enough—to satisfy customers, be profitable, and build the company to sell.

What Do You Know?
And, How Quickly Do You Know It?

Tracking is essential to success and we tracked *everything*. Inbound calls, outbound calls, talk time, conversion, transfers, follow-ups, sales, etc. The more, the better. Find your ultimate goal (number of sales, or dollars) and break that down into all the necessary steps and track each of those. We set daily, weekly, and monthly targets and pushed/compensated folks to hit them. Today, data is everything. If you can present a data-driven business, you will help its valuation.

Your range of sales reps will vary widely, and each might have different motivations. Mostly it's about money, but not always. Some will be great and strive to achieve/overachieve, and some will be slackers who will do the bare minimum. If they are profitable employees, let them be. Profitable employees are hard to find. You won't be managing clones. We're still a long way from AI robots replacing real salespeople. You'll be managing 3, 30, or 150 different, unique individuals, trying to get them all using the same oars and rowing in the same direction.

Train them, but the golden rule is *drill them*. Practice does make almost perfect, and the more you drill, the better they get. It's also a form of testing and accountability.

Unfair Sales Management

As a general rule, I tried to get my best leads to my best people. This pisses some people off. Fire them. You are in it to make money, and the best way to make money is to make sure your most valuable leads are being worked by the best sales reps.

Your slacker reps typically have an attitude personified by something like this: "Hey, Carlos, what's your goal today?" Carlos will say "five" or whatever the manager assigned him. "Great, are you going to get after it and hit your goal?" Carlos responds, "Well, depends on the calls. If I get enough good calls, maybe." Loser talk. You have to watch and worry about this guy. His bare-minimum, laissez-faire approach can be contagious. He might be productive enough to keep, but I'd be looking for his replacement every day. Under no circumstances should you bow to some idea of fairness or equity, and divvy up leads equally or at random.

Countless times I have walked to a sales rep's desk and asked them who they are going to close today. Occasionally I'll get a response of, "Well, I called Mr. Smith twice but he won't answer the phone." I'll grab the lead, pick up the phone, dial the number, and magically Mr. Smith answers. You would think they lied about attempting the call, but they didn't—they were being honest. The little-known secret here is intention. I intend to reach Mr. Smith and I do. Carlos or whoever intends to make or take a call, and he believes the outcome is out of his hands. Most people will gloss over this section. It may be the most important paragraph regarding success in the book.

It's a sad sign of the times, but excuse makers, victims, and those who can't be responsible for anything rule the day. *It's not my fault; it's the lead's fault; the calls are bad; my manager is giving someone else the golden leads,* etc., etc.

Nothing can correct if you assign the wrong causality. If you are broke, or not doing well, or unhappy, or haven't accomplished your goals, there is only one person to blame for that. Not the government, not your neighbor, not the leads. You. You are to blame. The vast majority of people will blame something for their poor situation. It is hard to correct in a person. Those that can take responsibility for their situation will be far more likely to correct it than those that can't.

Hire the Coachable, Who Want to Win, and Develop Them

Hiring is investing. You are investing time and money and there is "lost opportunity cost." The cumulative effect of your hiring will affect your company's value. It's useful to try and calculate and assign a true cost (investment) number for your hires, so you take this seriously. Hiring can be very challenging. We have tried all types of different testing. All bullshit. We could not find a correlation with sales success. IQ testing would help, as smart people do better than dumb people at most things. But for some reason that's illegal. Past success is your best indicator of future success. Outside of that, hire as methodically as you can and fire fast. You never *know* until they are on the job.

With salespeople, you want at least these characteristics:
- A positive attitude about selling and about closing.
- A competitive spirit and desire to win.
- Ability and willingness to "play within a system."
- Coachability (not a know-it-all, set in his/her ways).
- Past success *in something*—proof of being an achiever.

Over time you will build a strong (not perfect) sales force, pay them well, treat them well. Push targets. Keep them sharp with constant drilling and practice. Be happy with their Good Enough (the over-, the average- and even under-performers). This will be a system, a compliant and productive team, and a winning culture to proudly show off to potential buyers of your company.

CHAPTER 6

Built to Sell REVENUE, PROFIT, STABILITY

by David Melrose

O nce you have nailed down marketing and sales, the next requirements for a company's salability are revenues and profitability. This is not a textbook on accounting or finance. But what I will tell you will be far more valuable. As a side note, you need to hire competent finance folks *early*. In my business, they were critical. The simple math equation is dollars in the door minus your costs equals dollars left to take home. Accountants get real fancy and make things super complicated, but it all comes down to the above. Ultimately, it is that simple number that is going to factor into the equation used to price your small to mid-sized company.

During the start-up phase, you will be focused on your main product and trying to make it profitable with the few marketing methods you have. In the beginning, you do want to watch your leads like a hawk, perhaps working them yourself or requiring real-time feedback on the results. This phase is critical and will take hyper-vigilance on your part. Response rate, sales conversion, revenue per sale, minus any refunds/cancellations will give you the information needed to expand your first revenue stream. As your sales grow and your confidence builds, you will use the funds to further expand your sales and then start split testing (as discussed earlier) to increase your efficiency.

Over time, you will need multiple streams of income from other products or services, cross-selling, upselling, and, depending on your business—renewals or recurring revenue to be big enough to interest most possible buyers. Size matters, so top-line revenue and top-line growth matter. A business just growing profits without growing revenue is suspicious. Actual decline may be hidden from view by cost-cutting or -shifting. Year-over-year revenue growth is definitely a factor in whether your company is ready to be offered for sale. But, unless yours is a giant tech company, you are not likely to be forgiven for surrendering profits for growth either.

Keeping a Lid on Cost Growth

The fantastic entrepreneur and author Felix Dennis says, "Overhead walks on two feet." Fact-check—true. Elon Musk overpaid for Twitter and fired 80 percent of the staff. Despite some minor glitches and long nights, Twitter, now known as X, ran just fine.

Every tech company, the military, our administrative government, every corporation is overrun with worthless (or worse) jobs. While these may be fine people, the jobs themselves are worthless and bring zero value and in many cases active harm to our goal of building a successful organization. It's something I learned from Dan decades ago, and used in my businesses, and

Elon Musk has proven it to the world. The book *Bullshit Jobs* by David Graeber is worth reading regarding this topic.

We ran lean and mean and did our best to make sure everyone stayed busy with legitimately valuable work. Occasionally the body count would grow and we would have to reevaluate everyone and their duties to make sure that each and every one was needed (compared to wanted).

One telltale sign is when someone complains of too much work. Often when an employee starts screeching this, paradoxically it actually means they do not have enough work. The usual routine is this: Employee Joe Blow really is productive about four hours a day, and keeps himself "busy" by using his phone to play games, doom scroll social media, pay his bills, scroll Tinder for dates, etc. Until one luckless day he is asked to take on some new responsibilities and the response over time becomes "I am soooo busy!" Which brings unnecessary attention to him. This is a red flag for me, as my experience has shown that this is typically a cry for "you are cutting into my four hours of free time." We start looking at statistics, call logs, emails, etc. Inevitably what we find is that this person is working a fraction of the day. Which helps us with the problem of "overhead walks on two feet."

You want a culture of productivity and accountability. Productive people are happy people. Slackers know they are taking advantage of you and ultimately aren't happy and will leave you anyway. You are actually doing them and yourself a favor by keeping everyone productive, or getting rid of them.

Having the Best Price Strategies

Part of driving profits is pricing. Most companies price their product or service based on their competitors, or worse, how they feel about the amount of money being charged. Actually, only the market is always right. Your product, its marketing, its selling all mix to influence how much people are willing to pay, then they decide and we should let them. Your job is to command the highest prices (and highest margins) you can persuade the market to bear. Your job is *not* to calculate reasonable or affordable or fair or competitive prices.

This is a game of trial and error, and you are going to have to test it and compare all the related stats (conversion, etc.) to make sure your price strategies are working. Warning: Your sales reps will not like having to charge more and can torpedo any potential success. There are ways to mitigate this. The easiest way is to start high and work your way down, tracking all the way. Almost the entirety of the advice you will ever get on this topic will be wrong. Dan's advice on this helped me very early in my career and he has several resources on the topic, including the *No B.S. Price Strategy: The Ultimate No Holds Barred Kick Butt Take No Prisoners Guide to Profits, Power, and Prosperity.*

Dan says that price is almost always more "elastic" than a business owner believes. That is certainly my experience, stretching our prices if compared to direct competitors, and in evaluating other businesses as a consultant. This is bad enough when it is just unnecessarily suppressing your income as an active business owner, but it is far worse when it winds up negatively affecting the base number(s) that the multiple for your buyout is calculated with.

Will It Withstand Stormy Weather?

This is THE question of many timid, risk-averse buyers: This business looks great now and in the past few years, but how will it look in different market conditions? Is it safe or risky? Why? The case you can make for your business' stability can be very important when selling it, especially if, as Dan describes in Chapter 3, you are selling Downstream, or as Stan Kinder discusses in Chapter 14, you are selling to an individual.

The stability of my company came from our consistency in marketing. We learned to never waver in our outflow of media-generating leads, no matter how tempting it was in lean times or, say, over holidays, when response rates took a beating.

As "eerie" as it will sound, there it almost a *mystical* aspect to this. Anytime we cut the marketing budget or otherwise tried easing up on the marketing gas pedal, it always took twice as long for sales to recover compared to what they had been. It was like we were being punished by the Universe! We never could find any other reason so we learned to keep our marketing steady or increasing, no matter what. In all the discussions tied to our sale, this was one of the things that seemed to impress our acquirer; they saw that we had a marketing *machine* that chugged along predictably, no matter the short-term changes in the market or economy.

What Will They Think When They See Your "Elves"?

People are your greatest resource and they need to be cultivated and nourished for long periods of time, sometimes years. As the saying goes, good people are hard to come by. Harder to find than to grow. Maybe it's worse now than ever. Based on our educational system and the current societal trends, I don't see it getting better anytime soon. I've recruited and hired a handful of folks who have stayed with me over many years and they have done the lion's share of the work. You are going to need a few to build and sell a company. One of Dan's favorite, often quoted CEOs, Lee Iacocca, talked about his "ten horses" that pulled the giant teams at Ford and Chrysler. Pay the vital people well, treat them well, be tough but fair, let them get on with the job at hand. Have high expectations. Once you have a few in your corner, success becomes significantly more likely.

During due diligence, in search of *instability*, your buyer is going to carefully examine your numbers, your products, your customers, your tech or production capabilities, and your people.

CHAPTER 7

How to Sell "Blue Sky"

by Dan Kennedy

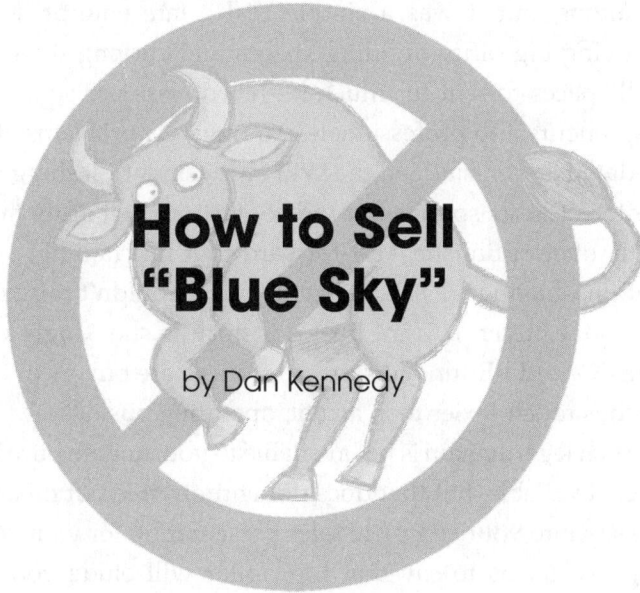

I n many respects, it *is easier* to sell a new, untested, unproven start-up company to investors than to sell a functioning one with actual performance results telling its story. Start-ups, especially in tech, get ridiculous valuations compared to existing, functioning businesses in the same space. This is because it's an imagined vision being sold, not facts. This can be very frustrating, but it points a way to a top-dollar selling price for the existing business: Add the allure of the start-up, diversification, or expansion that do not exist to the foundation of the business that does, as it is. Then you can use a valuation built from factual numbers *plus a valuation based on "blue sky."*

You will be told by most brokers, lawyers, and CPAs that this is ridiculous. But *they* aren't going to buy your company.

In its pre-revenue, idea stage, WeWork raised some $40 billion+ in venture capital. It was dumb. It got tech start-up valuations, but it was a simple real estate enterprise: leasing or buying big office building spaces and carving them up into small spaces to rent for much higher dollars per square foot to solopreneurs and professionals. Amongst its problems, it mostly pre-dated and misjudged the WFH Movement, slashing need for or interest in its spaces. But worse, virtually all of its math was wildly over-optimistic. Fast-forward to it functioning, operating locations, having a P/L statement, and it couldn't raise 40 cents, nor find a buyer. It went bust. Its story is shockingly common with VC- and PE-funded start-ups. These are buyers of blue sky, which is much sexier than actual, operating businesses.

Such legerdemain is not available to you, nor are pure blue sky buyers available, but that does not entirely rule out mixing some blue sky into your complete sales presentation for your company. I'll go so far as to say that top dollar will elude you without doing so. It's the space above formulaic valuation of only what presently exists in your business where the extra money waits. *The imagination* is much more price elastic than is the bean counter's analytical thinking limited by some "standard" formula.

Four Types of Blue Sky

There are four chief kinds of blue sky you may mix with an existing business: expansion, diversification, untapped revenue opportunities, and a coming breakthrough soon to be available.

As expansion, consider the successful chain of the restaurants or retail businesses or service businesses. If the owner continues opening one new company-owned unit each year, that's one thing. If the (new) owner were to keep only the home state for company units and franchise in the other 49, a business plan for that franchising can be prepared and presented. Instead of going from 3 to 4 to 5, it might go from 3 to 30 to 300. Ray Kroc never even bought the McDonald brothers' hamburger stand; he bought the franchising rights. One small, regional, family-owned pizza chain I'm familiar with (but can't name here) was bought by a PE-backed group for this exact reason—to use it as the model for national, then international, franchising. You see its TV ads constantly now. The original owners were paid about 3X what the business was worth as-was, based on its revenues, profits, and other facts. They also got a 1 percent royalty on all the franchise fees for 10 years after the sale. They got *very* rich.

Keep in mind that expansion is different than growth. The projected growth of the chain of bagel shops in the Cleveland area by growing their revenue, by better marketing, by opening earlier on weekdays, by adding products—like Starbucks did— is one thing. But the cloning of the group of shops in another city, Columbus, and another, Cincinnati, and the creation of an e-commerce business shipping Cleveland Bagels to Clevelanders relocated all across the country, adding a wholesale business, that's expansion.

As diversification, consider a client of mine with a big, successful national sales organization in the Medicare supplement plans field. They have perfected affordable lead generation by multi-media advertising, and perfected in-home appointment setting for agents. As of this writing, I am beginning work with them to use this exact same "machine" for two relatively simple, basic insurance and investment products. If we can succeed, we will have an extremely powerful proof-of-concept and, if they want to sell their company, a huge amount of blue sky to sell. If they prove that the same customers their operation sells Medicare supplements to will buy another financial product and/or they prove their entire system of lead generation advertising and appointment setting can be used for a different financial product with new customers—there are a dozen other financial products that could be sold that same way. To be simplistic, let's say there are 12 and there is a potential buyer for their company that deals with all 12, and they are doing 2. You 6X their revenue and profits to get to a blue sky number, but that's just the beginning. There is their first-to-market dominance, the ready-to-use (no building) nature of their "machine," and their expertise to sell. They'll likely be selling upstream to companies bigger than theirs, with no problem financing the purchase. This is why, instead of working on growing the business they already have, we are turning our efforts to cloning it to prove a big blue sky opportunity.

Incidentally, look at what DoorDash and Uber Eats have done. They started out just delivering food. Once conquering those delivery logistics, they began delivering darn near *everything*. This facilitates much higher value of each acquired customer.

For untapped revenue opportunities, we can use the company I sold. We had hit a brick wall. A lot of growth was possible with no new invention, but it would require having and managing a bigger staff than my tiny team. This was a Rubicon I did not want to cross. I could do it. I once had over 40 employees. I've helped countless clients with staff recruiting and management issues. But I simply didn't want to do it or manage someone doing it. I was dragging my feet, holding back growth begging to be unleashed. It was easy to show it.

Nowhere has this been illustrated more than at Disney. Eisner, then Iger, turned on one untapped revenue source after another, inside the Parks, for good or bad, starting with serving alcoholic beverages at restaurants inside the Parks, a longtime taboo. Converting one inclusive price to four different price tiers on a price pyramid. The list is long and it continues.

If you have untapped income sources and a reasonable explanation for why you haven't or won't tap them, but an explanation of how a different owner could, you have blue sky to sell.

In my case, one of these things was inbound and outbound telemarketers. There was no question that adding a telemarketing team would produce a big multiple of its cost. The thought of managing salespeople made me ill. The buyer had salespeople in his other companies, didn't mind it; *heck, liked it*. It was like adding booze to the restaurants in the Parks. It was as obvious as a big red truck parked in the middle of a frozen lake on a dull, gray winter day. It hadn't been done because Walt hated and feared it (even though Walt was a drinker). For a time after his death, the leaders were very reluctant to monkey with any of Walt's traditions. The ghost of Walt stood in the way of revenue begging to be unleashed. With my business, I stood in the way of revenue begging to be unleashed, for no good reason but my personal preferences. The buyer could see that, and could do the math. He would make the company produce more income almost instantly. It would be worth more in his hands than in mine, immediately.

For a coming breakthrough, the sale of my own company is a good example again. "Internet Marketing" was just emerging as an area of great, yet unknown, fast developing opportunity. It was perfectly matched with my business. It was easy to foresee a big increase in our size, speed of growth, and revenues by use of online media as well as opportunities to reduce costs. It was unimaginable that the company wouldn't at least 2× to 4× in the coming 24 to 36 months. I saw it and understood it, but personally wanted nothing to do with it. I didn't welcome the learning curve, and as noted just above, I didn't want to staff for it. There was going to be a revolution in our industry of information marketing and success education, but I wanted to sit it out. A buyer willing to run toward and embrace what I wanted to run from would be stepping into a ready-made, massive opportunity.

As I write this, "AI" is the big new thing. If I put a big sign that said AI TRASH.COM on my trash and put it out at the curb, it'd all be gone before the trash guys got there the next morning.

There is a crazed FOMO frenzy. There is also some legitimacy to it. A great many businesses will be made more efficient, cost-efficient, and more able by AI. If I were selling a company or a health care practice today, I'd have a little stack of articles from my trade journals and other sources supporting a brief document, like "Seven Ways AI Can Grow This Business," possibly written by an AI expert paid for that purpose. Behind AI, there'll be another Next Big Thing. And another.

Let me close here by being very blunt. Dull-witted, unimaginative professionals involved with selling small businesses, practices, and mid-sized companies will price and sell a company for a normal and customary multiple of gross or EBITA plus goodwill and hard assets. Even successful ones may be stuck inside this box. Sellers of companies who succeeded by these formulas know only these formulas. It all happens inside a box that favors the buyer. But there is no law saying you must stay in the box. You can find a buyer who will throw the formulas out entirely by your persuasion and work inside a different box you construct. You can find buyers who will agree to additional premiums added to the formula, uniquely for your business. Selling blue sky is one way to do that.

CHAPTER 8

The Secret of Magnetic Attraction of Your Buyer

by Dan Kennedy

We started out as a tribe of hunters. Cavemen got up every morning, shouldered a big, heavy club, and bravely went out in search of dinner. Fast-forward all the way through the 1950s and professional selling was still, largely, about *Eat What You Kill Today—Kill What You Eat Today*. Primitive. When I began promoting what I call Magnetic Marketing® in the late 1970s and early '80s as a replacement for hunting, cold prospecting, and primitive selling, and an alternative to brand advertising, I was a heretic in many circles.

The concept of magnetism in place of manual hunting, chasing, and dragging is actually quite ancient. The "law of attraction" has been a staple in the metaphysical world since at least the turn of the century. Books like *Mental Magnetism* thrived in the '30s and '40s. In the '60s, the immensely popular Dale Carnegie Program, extrapolated from his best-selling book *How to Win Friends and Influence People*, was about making yourself more appealing and interesting to others—more magnetic, without the word being used. So, I didn't invent anything or bring forward anything new under the sun, yet in sales industries, in advertising, with small business, it was looked at as radical and revolutionary.

With the selling of companies, most owners, most brokers, most M&A consultants are still stuck in Flintstones® land, doing quite primitive hunting. Language like "taking a company to market" is commonly used, while "attracting buyers to a company" is not. Hunting suppresses price. Attraction increases price. If you want to exit with top dollar, you should seriously consider a Magnetic Marketing®/Attraction Strategy. This requires thinking about what creates magnetic attraction so you can imbue your business with it.

Fame is magnetic.

Making yourself and your company broadly famous is no easy task.

The Taylor Swift "Secret"

In 2023–24, Taylor Swift alone accounted for 2 percent of all music sales in the U.S.—and that IS a lot. Yet she accounts for 50 percent+ of all the music-celebrity news. She has been *inescapable*. She is *daily* news. Without buying an ad, she was the most advertised "product" of the Super Bowl. Shortly before it, she made national celebrity, mainstream, and business news thanks to the mass circulation of deep-fake, AI-generated sexually explicit photos. *That* is a very good career move, so color me suspicious. She's having real sex with a famous NFL player, likable guy, who appears in dozens of TV ads, and has kind of a Paul Bunyan look going. This, too, is a good career move. At the Grammys, the ONLY artist EVER to get Album of the Year for the fourth time, she announced her "surprise" new album. Brilliant timing. Free ad during the Grammys. Announcement then repeated for her on every TV station, news broadcast, and social media when acknowledging her award. **But here is the most important lesson: With ALL that and being Her, she has only 2 percent of the product category sales.** It takes a mountain of "news" to filter down to a relatively small amount of actual consumer purchasing. It takes a mountain of exposure in any media, offline or online, by any means, to produce a small amount of book sales or album sales or buyers to a website. To get a single glass of juice, you have to shove a whole orchard into the juicer machine (along with a trout—*SNL* ref.).

To your market, you must "do Taylor Swift": One, you must be there, making news DAILY, and two, you must be inescapable. Unlike her, you probably need to define a market/audience small, tight, and reachable enough that you can afford being there daily, and being inescapable. But you *must* do those two things. Anything less and you can be ignored, you can be shoved aside by Taylor and others who DO get this, even made invisible and forgotten. Oh, and if you do this right, it'll bring out some haters. Just shake, shake, shake 'em off.

Making yourself and your company broadly famous is no easy task. But making yourself and your company famous in a narrowed, well-defined niche environment like a locality or a specific industry or profession or in a media can be very doable.

Here is the right idea: I don't need everybody to know my company. I only need its potential buyer to *believe* everybody does.

If you are very visible, ever-present, prominent, and talked about within a "place" where potential buyers of your company reside—such as an industry and its trade association and publications—you can bring buyers to you, inquiring of your possible interest in selling. *You won't have to hunt.*

You get to start with the potential buyer asking you out on a date instead of you being the one asking. This can be very important. Positioning matters. Being hard-to-get can motivate buyers. Being able to say, "Well, gee, I really wasn't thinking about selling anytime soon," is a whole lot better than saying, "Hey, I'd like to sell." I'd rather be asked than be asking, solicited than soliciting.

In your few years' run-up to when you want to sell, some time, energy, and money spent on this can be smart, even if its direct ROI is questionable. Full-page ads every month in a trade journal, for example, may not pay back 100 percent of their ad costs with new customers, but they do elevate you in perceived size, status, and success, and cause curiosity with competitors, peers, and possible buyers. Even PE active in an industry notices. Writing a book, getting it published, and heavily promoting it, even if you have to personally underwrite it, can get you and your company noticed. In short, when potential buyers look around the lake you are in, you want to be the shiniest fish they will want to pursue and catch.

Today, in a lot of business categories, social media presence and activity, and numbers of followers and likes and views, are used to judge the significance and potential of a business. Frankly, a lot of this is *silly*. Nevertheless, your potential buyers' perceptions are a reality. If you have not had this as a seriously attended-to part of your business, you may want to focus on it as you move toward the time when you want to sell. The redesign of company websites and the documentation of results is something you might look to The Internet Agency for help with, run by my client and friend Chris Cardell. Or look at AmericanEagle.com. Or eLaunchers.com. Media you may have done just fine ignoring, be it TikTok, YouTube, Instagram, Rumble, etc., may now need to be reconsidered because of the perceptions of potential buyers of your business. It isn't just what actually fuels your business and its good numbers that matters; it's what potential buyers *believe* to be important. There are two books in this series that can inform: *No B.S. Guide to Direct Response Social Media Marketing*, co-authored with Kim Walsh Phillips, and *No B.S. Guide to Successful Marketing Automation*, co-authored with Parthiv Shah.

CHAPTER 9

Will You Survive the Deal-Killers?

by Dan Kennedy

I f you read Robert Ringer's original *Winning Through Intimidation* book, or its remake as *To Be or Not to Be Intimidated* (and you should), you will discover his brilliant description of Deal-Killers, born of his painful experience.

In many cases, these can include the CPA, the lawyers, key staff, spouse, or family. In some cases, all of them surround your buyer to peck, peck, peck at him, building up doubts and worries, ultimately killing your deal. **The only defense is a preemptive strike.** You have to be the one to raise the concerns and objections and reasons not to buy that these Deal-Killers will produce. You have to be there first. You have to raise the issue, tell your buyer that his CPA or his attorney or his spouse is likely to say "X," explain why they'll see "X" as they do, and explain why they are wrong about it. Then, when his CPA pounces on "X," your buyer says to himself: "Wow. That's exactly what Bill Seller said my CPA would question—and he's wrong," and your buyer will also know how to answer his CPA, scripted by you.

Every business, no matter how appealing a dog, has some fleas. Every deal, no matter how great, has a few *uglies*. No business being sold is perfect or it probably wouldn't be for sale at a price any buyer could afford. To pretend otherwise and hope your buyer doesn't notice the fleas 'n flaws is foolish. If he doesn't, a Deal-Killer will.

Most professional advisors to a business buyer have no incentive to bless the deal and every incentive to kill it. They gain nothing by telling your buyer to go for it. If anything turns out badly, they'll be blamed for bad advice. They win by finding reasons to "protect" their client from the deal. *That* is what you are up against.

There are five counters to this:

1. **Preemptive strikes**, as I described above.
2. **Having a highly motivated, eager buyer.** You don't want to waste your time with the skeptic questioning everything or the person incapable of making their own decision, without bringing Deal-Killers in from the git-go. You want somebody who will decide, then instruct his lawyer to draw up or review and OK the paperwork and instruct the CPA to provide tax-related guidance. In short, you want to sell to an entrepreneur, if at all possible. If your company is too big for that, you at least want a situation where there is ONE key point-person driving the deal, backed by a big company or PE group or other investors. If you have a collection of potential buyers to figure out, you should consider this in ranking them, and determining who to approach first. And consider the value of your time and sanity, and the costs of disruption to your business if you engage in many months of the possible buyer's team's due

diligence with his people parked in your offices, prowling through every record, asking daily for another item, interviewing key employees. If, at the end of all that, their decision is "No" and you have to start over, consider the harm that has been done. The easier, faster sale, even if at 80 percent of your hoped-for price or at less perfect terms than you wanted, can be better than the one at 95 percent and desired terms if it takes a year, harms the business, and drives you crazy.

In the first sale of my Inner Circle company, I had a highly motivated buyer, an entrepreneur, a sole decision-maker. He had two successful businesses, one a "mini-me" of mine in the niche of his first business (menswear retailers), and he wanted to play on a much bigger stage, where my company was. He was chafing at the bit to do that yesterday. He was a customer/member and a client of mine, so we had a preexisting relationship. He could and would make a quick decision with nominal due diligence. I opened the door conversationally while we were at the Preakness together. He followed up almost immediately. We got to a completed deal painlessly, in weeks. For the second sale, by him, with me tagged on, fee and upside sharing by separate contract, he attracted a highly motivated buyer. A stranger, brought by an M&A broker. The broker found three potential buyers in about a 6-month search, brought two of the three to the table for serious discussions. One was cautious, the other was eager. She had recently exited a business as its CEO, and was rattling around loose, restless, and not drawing her CEO paycheck. She was an entrepreneur with PE backing. She could make solo decisions, then go sell what she wanted to do to them. Frankly, they did poor due diligence. They only met with and asked questions of me once, over lunch, despite my being an obviously vital component. The PE group did not understand what they bought. This should *not* be surprising. Just because people have or are managing a lot of money, does not mean they have a lot of smarts.

The third sale of the company was to another PE group, who bought at a near "fire sale" price. The owners had damaged the business badly. Some of the debt they piled onto it was borrowed from PE group #2, so they were stepping in to protect their money, assuming they could financially reengineer it, put a "professional" manager in place, and salvage their investment plus get in, fix, and get out with profits in short order, like buying, rehabbing, and flipping a house. I've never met people managing the amount of money they were, capable of making so many bad assumptions! This sale was quick and easy, but it did not work well. Soon, the fourth sale took place, again to an eager, motivated buyer who I brought in. He was an entrepreneur, with a successful synergistic company that should marry well with the one I was still attached to, he could make solo decisions, and we had a preexisting relationship. From start to finish, the sale from PE group #2 to him was completed in 3 months. This turned out to be a troubled marriage, too, and the fifth sale was from him and his publishing company to another entrepreneur I had mentored and coached and his big, $150 million software company. The reconstituted No B.S. Inner Circle business and its MagneticMarketing.com, with publishing, membership organization, online training, coaching groups, and events is, now, very happily married and thriving as never before at ClickFunnels.

Without eager, motivated buyers, somewhere on this journey there might have been no deal, no buyer, no influx of capital, and the business might have died.

There are always super-motivated buyers. I have a client who recently sold a large portion of a parcel of land he owns in Las Vegas, with good road access and frontage, close to the Raiders' stadium. He sold to Elon Musk. There was very little negotiation, the sale was completed quickly, and a price totally satisfactory to my client was paid. Why? Because "X" marks the spot for Musk. That land parcel is exactly where he needs to put one of his stops and passenger stations for his big underground tunnel that zips people around in Teslas. My client, by the way, got something out of this deal, more than the money: All the rest of that land could be sold and the buildings on it leased at instantly raised prices because Elon Musk had bought in, and because Musk's Loop Station would be there. My client got a celebrity endorser free. His sales letter going out to brokers, investors, and potential lessees was rewritten, starting with this headline:

What Does ELON MUSK Know About
Las Vegas Real Estate—*That You Don't?*

My client didn't have to give price or term concessions to use Musk in this way, but he could have and still made a very good sale. Musk could have negotiated for consideration and gotten it, but he didn't. I doubt it occurred to his deal-makers and he probably wasn't personally paying attention.

Whether found or not, there are always buyers with extra-perfect reasons to buy your company (or real estate or IP).

3. **Having, or having the appearance of, competitive buyers, creating FOMO, an auction mentality.** The possibility of not getting something you are interested in because somebody else beat you to it is a powerful psychological

force. I have owned racehorses for 20 years or so and I've been to a lot of racehorse auctions, and I owned a handful of classic cars and attended those auctions (which you can see on cable TV; look for Mecum Auctions)—and I have witnessed the "auction mentality" in others and felt it in myself. The created urgency affects the price you are willing to pay.

4. **Making the purchase a great bargain specifically for the buyer at hand.** For many years, Donald Trump had a right-hand deal-maker, George Ross. I brought George in to speak at my conferences several times, and got to know him well enough to get frank answers to my curious questions about working for and with Trump. George finished most of the real estate deals that Trump started. He said that Trump put together the purchase and the deal conceptually and with the seller, negotiated the big concessions, shook hands, and then left it to George to, as he put it, color inside all the lines. George said his mission was very clear: get the deal done. Contract written, signed, sealed and delivered. He said that the longer it took, the harder it got, as more Deal-Killers surfaced and entered the room. He said half of his effort went to fending off the Deal-Killers. To keep renewing the seller's *enthusiasm for selling to Donald Trump*, a fantastic bragging-rights cocktail party story. Trump says he overpaid for all his best properties because he knew what he was going to do to make them much more valuable, starting with putting his name on them—which, at the time, was absolutely true; his brand added value made from thin air, not bricks and mortar. (There is a big legal battle going on about this at the time I'm writing this. Trump lost the case in New York and is moving forward with appealing its verdict.) **There's an important lesson in**

this: **If you can help your potential buyer see a picture of all that he can do—that you haven't yet done, for various reasons—to dramatically speed growth, improve profits, or increase the business's value, you get to lean into *that* value rather than the actual, current, formulaic valuation of your company.**

The grand trick is to make the purchase free. This is often possible when there is synergy between the buyer's other business(es) and yours. I'll give you two examples. In one case, my client's company had about 100,000 responsive customers with profound interest in a particular recreational activity. Even though the company was not profitable, it could be with better management, and it had this asset. This list was closely guarded, never on the list rental market. The buyer had a new product about to be released from his company that these customers would crawl across broken glass, naked, to be the first in their club or group of friends to own, and get at a discount. I forecasted results from a "Top Secret" campaign to those 100,000 customers to produce a minimum of 2.5 percent (average for a house list) to twice that, 5 percent; 2,500 to 5,000 orders, at an $895 price point: $2.2 million to $4.4 million. Campaign cost of $500,000, cost of goods $375,000 to $750,000. Gross Profit to be $1.3 million to $2.6 million. The seller only wanted $3 million for his company (which, arguably, was worth less than $1 million). Structured at a cash purchase price of $1.5 million plus another $1.5 million from royalties tied to this promotion and future cross-selling between companies, the deal got done, fast. The promotion brought in just under $3 million. Repeated, as a "Last Chance" campaign, it brought in another $1.2 million. The buyer got the company *free*. Case #2, a company having a couple of different products manufactured for it by a small manufacturer (with a few other accounts, all profitable) was spending about $300,000 a month with the vendor on which the vendor had a 33 percent margin, $100,000. $1.2 million a year, gross profit. The vendor's client bought his company for $4 million, cash. They financed the purchase with a monthly payment of about $65,000 entirely paid for by the margin in what they were spending, with money left over. The purchase was free.

Sometimes, a savvy buyer finds a company to acquire that performs one of these kinds of tricks. The buyer knows how he can make a good acquisition free, and goes hunting for it. One might find you, with his scheme for free acquisition fully formed. Of course, a leprechaun riding a unicorn may show up on your birthday with cake, ice cream, and a pot of gold. Waiting for this to happen and/or counting on a potential buyer to figure these things out for himself is very unwise. You should take this responsibility.

Again, a Trump reference. When he originally purchased Mar-a-Lago, he had a "secret scheme" in mind to very quickly extract a lot of the purchase price out of the property—it was filled with exquisite, very valuable antiques, furniture, and art included in the deal. Trump had exceptional replicas made to stay in Mar-a-Lago and sold the real goods, for a great deal of money. If he had been the seller, he might well have, as quietly as possible, sold off the art and antiques and replaced them with replicas, pocketed that cash, then sold the property, disclosing the replicas, included. He might well have sold for the same price he paid.

The previously mentioned deal-maker for Trump reveals a lot of strategy in his book *Trump Strategies for Real Estate: Billionaire Lessons for the Small Investor*, well worth reading.

With all this, I'm championing the power of creative imagination to see what others don't see, to *create* math they don't know, to find hidden money, and to increase a buyer's desire and urgency. Walt Disney was often wrestling with his brother Roy over his grandiose projects. Roy was big on the question of: Where is this money going to come from? Walt said, "There is no shortage of money. There is only a shortage of imagination."

5. **Rapport and relationship.** If you are fortunate enough to be selling your business to somebody you have some preexisting relationship with, your project can be much easier. Whether a key employee, vendor, peer in your industry, or even a direct competitor or a family member, you start with some rapport, hopefully some trust or at least good reputation, some goodwill. This suggests the strategy of nurturing such relationships during a 3-to-7-year lead-up to taking your company to market. If there are possible future buyers you don't have a relationship with—such as an industry peer or maybe a successful entrepreneur in your community—go out of your way to get to know those people. To cultivate them for no apparent purpose or agenda. To "butter 'em up!" If I'm making myself a piece of toast and the butter stick in the fridge is rock hard, I set it on top of the toaster while the bread toasts, so I have warm, soft butter to use when my toast is ready. Same idea here: Warm 'em up *before* you are ready to ask them to be toast. If a potential buyer is raised by discreet advertising or by a broker or M&A firm, you start with the disadvantage of being a stranger. You should do what you can to change *that*. All business is really personal. Ultimately, people are much more likely to do business with, make concessions to, and get a deal done

faster with someone they know or at least know of, like, respect, admire, and trust than with a relative stranger or a big, impersonal entity.

A helpful resource is my book *No B.S. Trust-Based Marketing*. In it, you'll find guidance on accelerating the establishment of trust, why and how people *really* get to trust, and how to create a sense of collaboration on the deal, not two alley dogs fighting over every piece of meat on a bone.

What Is "The Thing"?

Often, there is something very important, often more emotional than financial, to the buyer—and to you, the seller—that, absent trust and rapport, people keep secret to themselves. It's very hard to discern it. It could be the hinge of the entire deal. The first buyer of my Inner Circle business wanted to be me, but wouldn't say as much, as nakedly, even though we had a good relationship. He expressed it more as a concern about customer/member retention or defection, about their acceptance of him as on par with me. I laid out the 3-Year Plan for gradually raising his status, acceptance, and influence, complete with MY communicating that the reduction of my leadership was by MY wishes, not me being pushed aside disrespectfully. Without going so far as stating it, the Plan basically made him, me. It included him becoming the author of a series of published books—I had NO B.S.; he would have OUTRAGEOUS ADVERTISING, then OUTRAGEOUS MARKETING, etc. It included him taking many of the speaking gigs I had been taking. And so on. Without selling this Plan, I might not have sold the company, or I might have had resistance to my asking price and terms. Without rapport and trust, I probably couldn't have sold The Plan!

A Prevailing, Majority Negative Response Is Unimportant—You Only Need ONE

Selling your company is not at all like selling a product or service. You are used to doing that. That requires making something appealing to a lot of people, if not a majority of a target market, or to the general public. That requires countering its every "negative" and focusing everybody's attention on the "positives," often involving the same kind of distraction that magicians use to get everybody watching their beautiful, sexy assistant in the skimpy, shiny costume climb into the box so nobody sees the back of the box being pushed out for her escape. That can't work when selling a company because you are nearly obligated to full transparency and disclosures, and you are open to due diligence—the buyer, accountant, lawyer all walking around to inspect the back of the box. This sounds bad, but it is nearly irrelevant, because you only need one willing "customer." One hundred of his peers can all look at your company and see it one way, the same way, but you only need one to see it differently.

There's even better news. There are entrepreneurs and conglomerates and investors who pride themselves on seeing things differently than the majority of their peers. There are buyers hunting for opportunities others miss or misunderstand. In Chapter 14, Stan Kinder gives an example of this, with the differences in what an individual dentist buying a dental practice can and will pay vs. what a PE-backed DSO group can and will pay...for the exact same practice.

As a relatively small investor in publicly traded companies, I balked at buying stock in Amazon or Apple for a fairly long time. But ultimately, I made over $1 million in gains on each, buying at a bargain during a "dip," because new facts changed the way I saw these companies. I switched from seeing Amazon as an online retailer to seeing it as "Google® for buyers," the search engine for consumers ready to buy things. I switched from seeing Apple® as a telephone maker and tech company to a utility and a holistic ecosystem holding users captive. It even took Buffett a long time to break free of his anathema toward investing in "tech," occurring by him seeing some tech companies as much more than tech companies. You need one buyer who can see the value of your business differently than most or all others do to successfully sell at top dollar.

What kills a deal for one buyer can be the thing that makes the deal with another. Everything perceived as a disadvantage by one buyer may be accepted as an advantage by another. In my case, for example, when I sold my company and later when that owner sold it with me still tagging along, the company was very personality driven. Its customers/members were attracted by and kept loyal by their relationship with me and him. Nothing we sold was a necessary utility. We weren't nameless, faceless IBM. We were two guys with strong personalities. The chief product— content; newsletters, courses, marketing tools, conferences—all featured us. With the second sale, to PE, several buyers were stopped by this. Fears about it were justified. But to the buyer, it was accepted as an advantage. It gave them "celebrities" they didn't have to hire and pay, continuity for customer retention after the sale, and, by contract, 3 years to ever so gradually and gently transition the business to being more institutional and corporate, with our suggested strategy. They felt the benefits outweighed the risks. We successfully sold what most feared as a lot of *added* value, above that of the company's assets and profits. Two potential buyers basically laughed at that idea. The third saw it our way.

With the first two, there were small armies of accountants, lawyers, and boards of directors, all Deal-Killers. With the third, there was one strong entrepreneur driving the deal with the PE group recruited by her, she was highly motivated, and she had more sway with the investors than their Deal-Killers did. They had done two business acquisitions and exits with her before and profited nicely both times, so her enthusiasm was good enough for them.

CHAPTER 10

My Top Five Lessons Learned

by David Melrose

1: The buyer is probably going to try to screw you any way he can. They may not have that intention at first, but it will develop, and you should expect to get worked over in the end. Due diligence in selling a business can take a *looonnnggg* time and is a lot of work. The bigger the buyer, the more resources they have to employ experts to analyze every little detail of your company. Initially you will be offered a seductively attractive deal, cash plus more money based on performance after you leave, profits, etc. Maybe they will offer you stock, which has a whole set of risks and not just with the stock price. You will be excited and think about all the nice things you are going to buy when the deal closes. Well, once they get done climbing up your back end with a microscope, that initial deal is going to be

discarded and accompanied with a whole bunch of justifications why the revised deal is significantly less.

If you are married to the deal and you and your spouse and family have "pre-spent" the money or planned your retirement and have mentally quit your business, you are in big trouble. You MUST stay insouciant throughout the entire process and until you sign and the money hits your account. (That's a big word and I'm not a big word guy, but it's the best one for this job. Look it up.) Their hope is that you have already quit and have one foot out the door, that you will take whatever offer they give you at the end. On top of that (and this advice I did get), expect them to f**k you at the end, to manipulate the financials, to claim you have violated your agreement, anything to reduce your money. What to do? You have to negotiate more than what you would be happy with in the beginning, knowing that it will be cut near the end. You also have to be OK with walking away from the deal. They've invested a lot of time and money in you, and it's not so easy for them to walk. Mentally it will be tough, but if you can maintain your indifference, it can pay off.

#2: Breaking up is hard to do. You will have formed bonds and friendships and your life purpose might be wrapped up in your business. Statistics show that when people retire, their life expectancy goes way down. Work is important. If you get enough money to retire, you will need something to fill the void. If you have kids and they are still small, that will help. Personally, I spent most of my time with my kids while they were young, and by the time I sold my business they were mostly grown. So, I had a midlife crisis and I went to the police academy. I also train in Brazilian Jiu-Jitsu and take lots of vacations with the family. Even so, I still got bored at times.

New businesses are always an option, but a word to the wise—you can easily blow everything you have pursuing this path. Many people do. In fact, you can blow it all without starting a new business. Ted Oakley (see Chapter 16) has helped me through the transition to semi-retirement and has some great books on the subject. His basic advice was, *do nothing. For two years. Nothing.* You will be tempted; people will want money. You will have friends and family with problems that they want you to solve, with your money. I had two financial advisors at the time. The other one wanted me to put it all in the market in stocks and bonds. I'd still be down millions today if I listened to him.

Having a great team will pay dividends. You will need good attorneys, an accounting firm, an M&A firm, and perhaps a consultant or two. You need to find these people in advance of your decision to sell. Vet them, meet with them, and hopefully work with them to make sure you are making the correct decision. These people are going to be on speed dial for a year and having a good relationship with them will be extremely helpful. It will also save you a lot of money. It is good to have a few trusted advisors you pay, but who don't have conflicting incentives. My coaching from Dan Kennedy has helped a lot, and Dan turned me on to Ted.

Be conservative with your investments. Depending on how much you get when you exit, if it's enough to achieve your goals and maintain your lifestyle, do not get greedy and try to run up the score. Whatever you think you may be missing out on will never be worth risking in questionable ventures or investments. We would all like to be billionaires, but you will never be able to forgive yourself if you somehow blow it all (and a surprisingly high percentage do). Be happy that you never have to work again for money.

#3: Be you. Some people say money changes you. I don't think so. Maybe because I have made a good living for a long time, but I don't see it, and those around me don't see it either. They say money can't buy happiness. What money does do is enhance your quality of life and more importantly enable you to help your friends and family, and community. If you aren't paying attention, things aren't necessarily great out there and seem to be increasingly getting worse, fast. With money, you can make a difference, even if it's small. You don't have to change. If you never belonged to the fancy country club before, why do you have to now, just because you can? On the other hand, if that's something you always wanted to do, now you can—put on your tux and write the check.

#4: You are going to have a lot of free time. Continuing your education, spending time with your friends, taking up a new hobby (or better yet a new sport that requires a significant amount of exertion, lifting, boxing, MMA, BJJ) will do wonders for your mental and physical health. For myself, I got licensed as a private investigator, went to the police academy, and became a reserve deputy. I could have started multiple businesses along the way, but my non-compete runs three years and nothing would have been as profitable, and anything would have had some risk. For what? Some extra cash? Don't need it. Why would I trade time for dollars? Time is, of course, your most valuable asset. Spend it wisely.

#5: Relax. One thing I learned is how much stress you are really under when you have to work for money and are self-employed. Although I worked only a handful of hours a week, my mind never quit. 24/7, 365 days a year. You are always on the clock. Your life is just one moment away from becoming a disaster. Now that I am on the other side of it, it's certainly a nice feeling, and I was able to really relax for the first time in a long time. Be OK with that. You earned this, and don't let anybody tell you differently—not Bernie Sanders or President Biden or the media or, I hope not, your kid you are putting through college.

Ultimately, if you decide to do it all over again, as I have, that's fine—it's your choice, and you earned that choice, too. Do it smarter, faster, more confidently, and maybe pace yourself to enjoy it more the second time around.

CHAPTER 11

Life, Liberty, & the Pursuit of Happiness AFTER the Sale

by Dan Kennedy

Eagerness to sell makes most business owners imprudent. Eager to overlook and neglect all sorts of details that they fear slowing or killing the sale if contested, and that they tell themselves just won't matter *to them*. Any one of these details may wind up controlling your liberty after the sale.

Quick note: I am about to talk about some legal stuff. I'm not a lawyer and I don't play one on TV. Please read the Important Notes on Page viii.

Swiss Cheese Non-Compete Agreement and Carve-Outs

You will be asked to sign a non-compete agreement, which, if the buyer has his lawyer write it, will be so broad and all-encompassing that you may not be permitted to walk across the street on Tuesdays for the coming 3 years. You CAN'T let yourself be wrapped up in one of these. Instead, you want a Swiss Cheese Non-Compete. One that gives the buyer the comfort of a very narrowly crafted pledge against your direct competition for the agreed-on term, but, but, but has lots of holes in it, just like a piece of Swiss Cheese.

My own agreement with the first sale of Inner Circle had a two-paragraph Non-Compete Agreement with three pages of specific carve-outs in an Addendum. These protected three things: preexisting activities that might be considered competitive—in my case, work with clients who used me as a co-author or endorser in niche markets that the Inner Circle business overlapped; activities I might want to do, that I could imagine, and write up in narrow and precise terms; and three, ideas for things I might offer to do with the owner and the company as joint ventures that I felt like disclosing. I took *days* working on this, to be sure I included every possibility. In the second and third sale of the company, each involving a consulting and services contract with me separate from the purchase agreement, the issue of non-compete always came up, and a revised version of my pages of carve-outs migrated to the new agreement.

Because I was careful, thorough, and forceful with this, in all the years, I never had one conflict of interest discussion or problem. When the first buyer was reselling to a second, I offered to help with his Swiss Cheese, but he declined, relied on his lawyer, and signed a blanket non-compete. In a matter of months post-sale, he was having difficulty after difficulty and deeply regretted signing it. He had, for example, occasionally taken copywriting gigs from clients who rose up out of the company's members/customers. But now, the new owners caught this and objected, demanding, at least, a percentage of the fees to allow him to do it. This could have been avoided.

Seasoned M&A attorneys have seen what I've done with this surgical dismantling of the non-compete cage and told me that "it's impossible." But my model for this has now been used by at least dozens of sellers of businesses that I know of. Tom Cruise has made *eight* Mission Impossible movies. At this point it's ironic and comedic to use the title. He's doing Mission Possibles. Difficult, yes. Involving amazing stunts, yes. But "impossible," nope. Same thing here. What the lawyers see as a Mission Impossible, you have to see as a real entrepreneur sees it. Say: Let's just find out what's possible and what isn't.

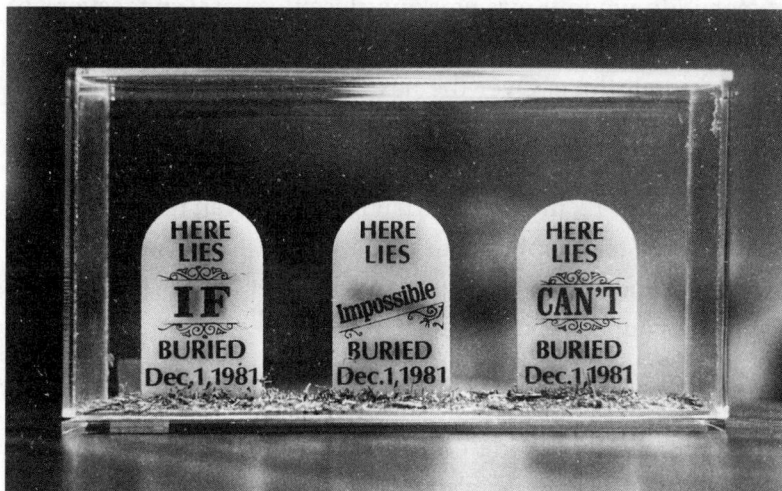

I buried "Impossible" along with two other "bad words" in an actual graveyard outside my offices in 1981. My favorite saying comes from movie mogul Sam Goldwyn: "It's an impossible situation—but it has possibilities!" Be sure not to accept the first "that's impossible" you get from anybody.

More to Get

There may be opportunities the business has, that it has not acted on, that are in your head and not on paper, and thus not part of the value determining the sale price. You should think about each one carefully. You may decide to throw it in, to help the "blue sky" portion of your value argument. This can be especially persuasive if it is synergistic with the buyer's other business(es). Or you may want to keep it to yourself, as something you bring forward later, post-sale, as a new joint venture.

There are all sorts of disclosures you must make that you'll either offer voluntarily or have raised by the buyer's due diligence, but you are NOT legally (or ethically) required to disclose what may be on your mind about yet only imagined opportunities! After my sale of my Inner Circle business, I later brought the new owner, with whom I was working closely, several suggestions of things we might do, outside the contract. I proposed three. He welcomed all three. Over the next 5 years, I made well over $1 million from those three ventures bolted on to and fed by the company he had bought.

In Chapter 12, my friend Brian Kaskavalciyan reveals how he "got his cake and kept cake to eat later, too." He closely followed my model and examples. Be sure to consider his story when you approach your sell/buy agreement.

As a general, broader observation, he who signs where the little yellow Post-it® note arrows are is almost always getting things slipped by that deserve at least careful thought, possibly negotiation. You should also adopt the principle that *standard, normal, customary,* and *just boilerplate* are for other people—not you. Personally, I prefer taking the notes from verbal discussion (a transcript if possible) and the skeleton of the agreement and then writing the agreement myself. I've done this for 50 years with countless author, consulting, business sales, and other legal agreements. I'd rather be looking at possible changes or corrections to my draft than fighting to get changes or corrections made to the other guy's draft. This also permits what I call *Alexander King's Gambit,* which I use a lot and rarely reveal, but will do so here.

Alexander King was a popular talk radio personality, I think in the '50s. I never heard him, but my grandmother gave me a paperback copy of his memoir. In it, he describes a time in his life as a "starving artist." He was talented but unable to figure out how to make money. He was living with a roommate in a tiny New York City apartment. His roommate got a job at an ad agency where a client, a major brand cruise line, wanted to have—instead of a photo—a magnificent artist's painting of 300 couples in formal attire dancing and partying on the top deck under beautiful moonlight. His roommate got the gig for King. King then produced an amazing painting matching the client's vision. Delivered to the agency, the executives praised it. It was put on an easel, covered in velvet, and the client was brought in, with King the Artist, the ad executives all present, champagne served. The painting was unveiled. Applause. Then the client's VP of Advertising closely inspected it, turned to King, and said, "It is exactly what we want but for one small thing. I think all the dancing couples should be turned a little bit to the left." Alexander King had a temper. He flew into a rage, grabbed the painting, tore it to pieces, and stormed out—still a starving artist. The agency's Art Director caught up with him at the elevator and said, "You are a fool. You painted a *perfect* painting. But that guy *has to* justify his existence. He *has to* find something to change. You should have painted a hairy man's arm on one of the women. He could have found that. You could have easily scraped it off with a razor blade and painted it correctly. But no, you idiot, you made the perfect painting."

Ever since reading that, in my teens, I've painted a hairy man's arm on a woman into every contract. I mean, an item I want them to object to, to focus their attention on, to negotiate away, that I can give in on seemingly sadly and with great reluctance. I have done this in sizable contracts with big companies like WeightWatchers®, Miracle-Ear®, Mass Mutual Insurance, and many more. I've done it in small business. It's never failed. They are so pleased with themselves to have spotted the hairy arm and make me fix it, they gloss over everything else.

This applies to conversational deal-making, too, not just the contract. In conversation, as you articulate the "top 10 list" of items important to you, throw in a ringer. Include an Ask that you are certain the other party, in this case the buyer, will find unacceptable and balk at. When you first mention it, give it some emphasis. For example, with a mid-sized company, you might say you want contractual assurance that none of your longest-tenured, key employees can be terminated or replaced for 36 months after the sale. The more your buyer focuses on this unreasonable and, to him, unacceptable item, the better. That'll mean he'll focus less on other items. No buyer ever pays full asking price and agrees to all requested terms, so *you* want to tee up the one or two you'll have to surrender. This gives your buyer a win, without giving you a loss. Use something you actually care little about, but can appear to care about a lot, and that he will certainly see leap out at him like the one hairy arm in King's otherwise perfect painting.

I have rarely told the Alexander King Gambit to audiences or clients. I'm only doing it now, here, so publicly, because I am at the edge of retirement.

Your New Job Description

Somewhat the other side of the NC and NDA agreements coin is the post-sale employment or consulting agreement. Something of a common norm is it is written for 3 years. That seems a short and therefore inconsequential period of time, but if you find yourself on the rack, in a torture chamber, 3 years can be an eternity. Three years is 1,095 days. It can be many painful days watching the new owners do remarkably dumb things. Worse, it can be many days of required participation in the dumb things.

The big error made here by sellers is with vagueness. Just saying that you will be available for "x" as needed puts you on call 24/7/365. Using a phrase like "will exert best efforts to" leaves open to dispute defining best efforts. ALL agreements with the buyer carry risk to you, of different interpretation, disputes, avoiding paying you agreed-on post-sale money, and lawsuits. It is up to you to reduce these risks.

The biggest hazard to avoid is "mission creep." This is doubly dangerous if you have back-end money tied to certain revenue, growth, or profit benchmarks. You now own schizophrenic conflict of interest, a fight between your desire not to do more work or put in more time than planned and not to be coerced or bullied into doing so vs. feeling you need to do more because they are a ship of fools and you have a payout to protect. One of two things typically occurs post-sale: Either you'll be asked to do a lot less than your employment agreement calls for or you'll be asked to do more. And more. And more still. The first may be an irritant to your ego, but it doesn't interfere with your life. The second one certainly does.

After the sale of No B.S. Inner Circle, from the buyer I had first sold to, an entrepreneur, with whom I then worked nearly like a partner, the second time to a private equity group backing an entrepreneur, we each had 3-year post-sale work-for-hire agreements. His lawyer wrote his. I wrote mine. His lawyer undoubtedly worked from boilerplate content and clauses. I worked from my paranoia about getting trapped in a bad marriage with no way out. He failed with his agreement twice. First, he had a solid non-compete; I had Swiss cheese. Second, worse, he had a vague, broadly, sloppily worded page describing his responsibilities. I had about three pages of very precise descriptions of my responsibilities. For example, his included "providing on-going advice" and "assisting with or, as necessary, writing advertising and marketing copy." Whoa Nellie! Advice about what? How delivered? In what time? Same with writing copy—as needed? How much is that? Who decides what's needed? The risk here of being asked for more and more and more time, for reporting to the office instead of working from home or his second vacation home, of being consumed, of—by this—becoming horribly unhappy, angry, bitter, then balking but with nothing in writing to make the balking legit—therefore—making the buyer angry…is no risk at all. *It's guaranteed!*

He had exited with a very large pile of cash plus "tails"—i.e., money yet to come—finally free of waking up every morning and putting on his track shoes to race a panoply of CEO responsibilities (or so he thought) to very quickly wind up *miserable*.

My agreement included advice-giving and copywriting. With the advice-giving, specific matters and limitations were listed, the means described—one pre-set, one-hour phone call each month, one extra, if-needed phone call, fax memos exchanged weekly. For copywriting, one project per calendar quarter. For each and every accepted duty, what I would and wouldn't do was thoroughly described. The footnote to it all was that if additional time and/or in-person meetings were required, additional fees would apply. During the 3 years post-sale, I can't claim I was beloved, but there was very little friction and no significant disagreements.

At the end of the whole multi-sale journey, there was a lot of bad blood between him and the buyers, including litigation. There was no bad blood between me and them, and I was paid the agreed-upon 3-year money plus more for accepting a bigger role. I never regretted my 3-year and then extended work-for-hire agreement.

What you want to take time to think through and write *tight* is the agreement governing what services, work, and time you will (and won't) provide during those 3 years. Specificity, even if surprising to the buyer and difficult to deal with during the sale, will be much, much more difficult to deal with later if left vague. Any honest lawyer will tell you that they get rich on *ambiguity* in contracts. If you don't want to hand a lot of your payout over to a lawyer handling post-sale litigation, avoid ambiguity like the China Virus.

Before You and They Say "I Do"

Somewhere, you will also want a prenup for the 3-year marriage that defines how they end it prematurely, and how you can end it prematurely. The time to negotiate your firing or your escape is when nobody is worried about it.

There may be different financial ramifications for your termination by them or an exit by your choice if "with cause" or "without cause." If so, "cause" has to be well-defined. Assume you are O. J. Simpson and you sold your sports memorabilia company about a week before the murders and the Bronco chase, and the buyer had you under contract for 3 years post-sale, with responsibilities including being a celebrity endorser. Oops. If the buy/sell agreement, the work-for-hire agreement, or a prenup had a morals and reputation damage clause in it, allowing the buyer to terminate your agreement(s) and compensation tied to your performing duties or even just being a celebrity endorser, he would terminate "with cause" and you, O. J., might lose out on a lot of money. Probably true even though you were ultimately found NOT guilty. However, if none of that was spelled out, the buyer might have to terminate you "without cause" and still pay you agreed-on, post-sale monies. I realize you aren't planning on killing anybody, and you and your buyer are holding hands happily at the altar. But life happens.

What Happens If They Can't Pay

In Chapter 13, Dr. David Phelps talks ruefully about the first time he sold his dental practice, with seller financing. It was what he calls a "boomerang sale." The buyer defaulted, the practice had to be repossessed and taken back. In *The Godfather*, Pacino, in the kitchen, cries, "Just when I'm almost out, they pull me back in." You can, of course, avoid this possibility entirely with a full cash sale. But a lot of small business to mid-size company sales involve some portion of the total price being seller financed. If this is in play for you, you need a long discussion with an attorney *specifically* knowledgeable about seller-financed deals. There are many issues. Defining default process for you getting business back as early, quickly, and cleanly as possible, remaining liability (if any) of the buyer, and how a bankruptcy filing by the buyer will affect you and your ability to reclaim the business (or, at minimum, terminate your non-compete and any other obligations to it). Even without problems, you want clarity about the transferability of the note should you want to sell all or part to an investor at a discount or transfer it to your offspring, siblings, or a charity. You may also want collateral in addition to the business, like a second mortgage on a buyer's home, or a co-signer, subject to release as payment benchmarks are met.

Seller financing can give you added profit from the sale, with a higher interest rate than obtainable from ordinary investments, and it can grease the wheels of a sale, but it is loaded up with peril. The attorney I know who is extremely knowledgeable and experienced with investing in and owning and selling notes and debt instruments, and with seller financing, is Laurence J. Pino. You can find him at PinoLawGroup.com.

SECTION TWO

INTERVIEWS WITH COMPANY OWNERS ABOUT THEIR EXITS

CHAPTER 12

Interview with Brian and Adi Kaskavalciyan

Sell Your Cake and Eat It, Too

DAN: Brian and Adi Kaskavalciyan are the founders of gFour Marketing, a marketing agency, and The Wealthy Contractor™, a training and coaching company in the home improvement contractor industry. I'm happy to say that "I knew him when," as they started with me when young and beginning in these businesses. In 2023, they sold their company—yet kept a desired part of the business, something we'll talk about here.

Brian, let's start with the story itself, just as background.

BRIAN: In 2009, we were in bad financial shape, with nearly a million dollars in debt as a result of making some really bad decisions in my previous businesses. We were losing our house and we were out of money. I was doing some random consulting work, and I was miserable. While working with a client who sold advertising to home contractors, I sketched out a "system" for developing the customer relationship *after* the job was completed, for referrals and future work. Frankly, most of that "system" came from you. I had learned from you about total customer value, and your principle: Most get a customer just to make a sale—we make sales to get customers for life. This was and still is foreign to contractors. In the industry, there is addiction to new leads, its cocaine. My client had no interest in bringing my ideas to his ad clients. A few weeks later, at my daughter's soccer game, another dad told me about a business he had just acquired that sent cookies to customers on behalf of auto dealers. He bought it because he owned the bakery that made the cookies, but he didn't know what to do with it, to grow it.

DAN: I'll interrupt you to make a point I've made elsewhere in this book. It might surprise people how many companies are acquired by owners with little or no creative vision for what to do with them after they get them. Happens all the time. That's why I urge sellers of businesses to present the creative vision for the business's future when they are presenting it as it is, for sale. Anyway, you put 2+2 together...

BRIAN: I thought this would be a great relationship builder for home contractors. Because of Infusionsoft (now Keap, a CRM/ marketing software), we were able to add other elements of a relationship system like a monthly email newsletter, quarterly print newsletter, customer surveys, all in a done-for-them service. As you know, the recurring revenue model was big in the Kennedy World at that time—an automatic monthly charge *for something*. We built three levels of done-for-you communication with a contractor's customers: Basic, Deluxe, and Premium. Later, we added a referral rewards program. Later, we saw Google Reviews becoming a big issue, so we added that—getting good reviews posted. We became THE "relationship marketing people" in this industry.

We were out of money when we started. The last asset we had was an insurance policy we were able to borrow $25,000 against. We bootstrapped this whole thing. A prominent contractor, Charlie, was on the first webinar I did, to sell what we called our "1 into 5 Program." He bought and became our champion. Within months of getting great results from our program, he introduced us to an organization of contractors and that really launched us. That also started my speaking career at industry conferences.

DAN: To be crassly commercial, you used three of the Wealth Magnets in my book *No B.S. Wealth Attraction for Entrepreneurs*: One, be Somebody; two, be Someplace; three, do Something. You were opportunistic. It's unfortunate for them that most people aren't. So, is this story that you then instantly went from dead broke to rich? I know that's not the case. Give us the progression.

BRIAN: The first years were slow. It took us 5 years to break $1 million, but we *were* profitable from the beginning. It gave us a decent living. In 2016, I started *The Wealthy Contractor*™ podcast. I got industry leaders and, of course, my clients on as guests. The speaking I'd been doing plus the podcasts established me as an expert, authority, and kind of a celebrity. We naturally moved into seminar events, following your model. That took on a healthy life of its own. Our most recent event had over 400 contractors at it. By 2019, Adi, my wife, and I had a good team in place—we were moving ourselves out of the day-to-day, and the business turned a seven-figure profit.

DAN: So, at that point, you had built sort of a two-headed monster: an agency business with the done-for-them services and a seminar and training business. Maybe not easy to sell. I have an interest in and consult with a very similar two-headed monster, The Internet Agency, in the U.K.

BRIAN: We were advised to separate the agency business from the information and events business. There was now enough revenue and profit to divide and still have great businesses. The information and events business had fueled the agency, but that was no longer necessary. It was thriving and growing on its own. We split the businesses. It may have been the best decision we ever made.

DAN: Why, when, and how did you sell?

ADI: It was always our desire to have a BIG exit, to create financial security for ourselves and our family. After losing everything in 2009, we just didn't want to have our wealth locked up inside one company. Brian and I had differed over the right time to sell. When he wanted to, I didn't. Vice versa. Then the day came when we both agreed on the timing. The split-off company, The Wealthy Contractor™, with information, events, and coaching, was growing and asking for more of our time. The agency had the recurring revenue, which we knew was a key to a big multiple. So, in 2022, we got serious about selling the agency.

By then, private equity buyers had invaded the industry and were buying up contractors; however, the company we were talking to was buying up tech and marketing companies that *served* contractors. They were combining the businesses— software for them, and services to them. PE acquired two top CRMs, a number of Internet marketing agencies, lead generation companies. In 2023, we met up with a PE group we had talked with a few years earlier, and been judged not ready. This time, we got into serious discussions with their acquisition team. I also had a good friend who had sold his company to this same group, and he introduced me to his investment banker. The possibility of selling to this PE group fizzled. They were in financial trouble themselves. But the banker brought us another candidate, a PE- and family offices–backed entrepreneur we immediately hit it off with, who understood the special value of our company and of us working collaboratively after the sale. Within a week, we had a good LOI.

DAN: You did good things. You were willing to walk away from a weak offer from a bad buyer. You didn't just sell the company as is. You presented opportunities. You got help—in this case, a good investment banker with experience in your industry. Now, let's get to the payoff. You guys did a brilliant job with the deal itself. Describe as much of it as you're willing.

ADI: The total value of the deal was eight figures, based on a multiple of cash flow. We received 85 percent of that in cash, with a small escrow paid out half in 90 days, half in 18 months, against certain contingencies. Ten percent was in a seller note. Five percent was rolled over into an equity position in the newly formed company, including ours. We *didn't* like this at first. We were selling to eliminate risk, period. But it became a deal-breaker. It has turned out very well. We have a board seat, and the board is composed of smart, professional investors. The entrepreneur-CEO has been fantastic to work with. We anticipate a 10× return on our investment within a few years. There was also a 12-month consulting agreement. We kept The Wealthy Contractor® business, separated before the sale.

DAN: That's your "sell the cake but eat it, too." I did exactly the same thing. Entrepreneurs need to understand that they can cut up and reassemble their company for sale, differently than it has been.

ADI: This business has information publishing, events, sponsors' fees for the events, and coaching and mastermind groups—and that has grown dramatically. Wealthy Contractor does not make a seven-figure profit YET—it will do about $2,000,000 in revenue this year. It is still fed partially by agency clients coming over, and we still refer in the other direction. In your terms, we kept the top of the pyramid and sold the bottom.

BRIAN: I think this had an extra benefit. We were not abruptly left with nothing to do after the sale. You've counseled how dangerous that is. We have the part of the business that we like best, enjoy, can operate simply, and be busy with.

DAN: What do you think made the biggest contribution to your sale and getting the price you wanted?

BRIAN: There is no doubt that having a recurring revenue model in the business made us an attractive acquisition. Our retention vs. attrition rate was impressive, something we obviously worked on. We showed solid year-over-year growth, our gross margins were fantastic, and profit was consistently above 30 percent. It was also noted that this was a very organized business. We had systems in place. A great team in place. During due diligence, they met with Adi, they met with team members, and they were blown away by our culture of accountability.

DAN: How do you feel about it all now?

BRIAN: I have often said that it is shocking that this little done-for-them marketing business that sold a concept and marketing people didn't want became a multi-million-dollar business, let alone a business that made me and Adi multi-millionaires in about 10 years, and then financially free just 3 years later. We've experienced many emotions. I would say that becoming rich is not easy, but neither is *being* rich. You have to develop new mindsets, new skills, and develop as a person. Your influence has, of course, been important every step of this journey. Now we are helping contractors become truly wealthy contractors, in part, by sharing our experiences.

BRIAN AND ADI KASKAVALCIYAN are the authors of *The Wealthy Contractor Blueprint Program™* and *The 7 Secrets to Becoming a Wealthy Contractor*, conduct mastermind groups, and hold seminar events. You can contact them at TheWealthyContractor.com

---

CHAPTER 13

Interview with Dr. David Phelps

Selling a Professional Practice, the Same Practice Twice, and Hard Lessons Learned

DAN: Dr. David Phelps is a coach, consultant, and mentor to dentists and other professionals on business, finance, and life transformation, notably through the sale of their practices and replacement of that income. He is the author of several books, including one I'm pleased to have co-authored, *Own Your Freedom*.

For decades I've had a sign in my office that reads ". . . but MY business is DIFFERENT." It's on the wall because everybody says it to me, when we talk about marketing, and I argue all businesses are fundamentally the same, and what works with any one business can be translated to work for any other business. I have found most entrepreneurs err in the other direction when it comes to selling their business. They think all are the same. There's a math formula and that's it. But I'm willing to hear from you why selling a practice—dental, like yours, other health care, law, CPA, etc.—*is different* from selling other kinds of companies.

DR. PHELPS: Professional practices are more difficult to sell than many other types of businesses because they depend on a key person: the owner-doctor. Whether dental practices, veterinary practices, or any other type of practice, they are typically very reliant on the doctor or professional practitioner for production and for patient or client retention. However, any business allowed to be so centered around and dependent on its owner-operator will run up against the same challenges with a sale.

Because of this, professional practice sales often don't get the same multiples as other businesses where the owner is not embedded in the heart of the business. This can come as an unhappy surprise to the doctor.

If the practice owner doesn't come to the table with a reassuring plan for the transition, for retention of patients, for keeping up the current level of production, he's going to find himself being pressured for price concessions. At the same time, if he doesn't have some of what you call "blue sky," a vision for growth, then all he's selling is equipment plus cash flow.

DAN: Are practices being bought? Who's buying them?

DR. PHELPS: There has recently been and there is major disruption and consolidation in private practices. Since the early 2000s, we have seen significant consolidation in the private practice arena as private equity seeks to commoditize entire industries. Their entrance into a market is accompanied by large-scale acquisitions of private practices at previously unseen multiples. Once, a dental practice was sold by an older dentist to a younger, up-and-coming dentist. From one individual to another. Then multi-doctor partnerships and multi-office practices changed who practices could be sold to. Now, Wall Street's private equity entities are in this space.

This creates new opportunities as well as new challenges for private practitioners. It often creates a window of opportunity to cash out for top dollar, but extra care must be taken when negotiating a deal with private equity. Most practitioners have little to no experience structuring such a transaction, and few have taken the time and effort to maximize the value potential of their practice in the marketplace. That was certainly the case for me. I had an urgency to sell, something you want to avoid if you can by advance planning.

DAN: Let's get into your experience, with the sale of your practice.

DR. PHELPS: It's called The Boomerang Practice Sale, because it leaves the owner but then comes back.

In the quiet moments of reflection, sitting beside my daughter Jenna in a hospital room, I found my life's trajectory irrevocably altered. I never envisioned an endgame for my career; I assumed I would follow in the footsteps of my father, an eye surgeon, and retire from dentistry in my sixties. However, life, as it often does, had other plans. Jenna's battle with high-risk leukemia at the tender age of two and a half threw our family into turmoil. Her illness and ongoing health issues, including epileptic seizures and eventual liver failure, forced me to reassess everything I thought I knew about my life and career. This meant that the decision to sell my dental practice wasn't part of a well-orchestrated plan. Watching Jenna fight for her life, I realized my place was beside her—not in a dental office. My financial stability from real estate investments suddenly took on a new meaning. It wasn't just a safety net, but my ticket to being there for Jenna when she needed me the most. Finding a buyer for my practice, as quickly as possible, became necessary—not just for financial reasons, but also as a step toward reclaiming my life and priorities. The process was far from smooth. The initial buyer was a promising candidate. He had credit issues—the first red flag, in hindsight—but I thought those issues were behind him, and I used my real estate experience to structure seller financing for the practice. It was a clever solution. Unfortunately, the credit issues were the tip of an iceberg of *character* issues that began to sink the practice. He was not up to the task. What followed was a drawn-out default and legal battles. Looking back, there were plenty of red flags, but I was a highly motivated seller. In that first attempt I took a rugged John Wayne individualist approach—thinking I could figure it all out on my own. I advise dentists I now coach, and other entrepreneurs I network with, to be very careful about being too highly motivated or too impatient. To watch for red flags. And to get knowledgeable guidance.

The practice I took back was in disarray, a shadow of the successful business I had once built. I had lost the trust I had spent years building with patients and staff. I faced a tough decision: shutter the practice and walk away, fire-selling it for a fraction of its worth, or roll up my sleeves and rebuild. I've never been one to walk away. But I am one to learn from my mistakes. This time, I sought advice from trusted mentors and guides. Dan Kennedy became one of my mentors. The path forward required letting go of the need to be the primary driver of my practice. I learned to be a CEO rather than just a dentist. This shift wasn't easy, but it was necessary. Fast-forward 3 hard years later, and I successfully sold my newly rebuilt practice for a very good price, to a stable, financially sound, capable buyer. I learned some painful and valuable lessons through that experience.

DAN: I think it was Alan Greenspan, talking about stocks and the stock market, who coined the term "irrational exuberance." It's easy to get irrationally or prematurely exuberant about the buyer in front of you, have the sale done in your mind, and then be very reluctant to undo it. Also, I see a lot of sellers, for no good reason like you had, decide to sell suddenly, and move forward fast, without taking time to prepare the business, themselves, or their absolute requirements not to be negotiated away.

DR. PHELPS: Owners of professional practices are very often workers in it rather than CEOs of it, and that says it's not a business ready to sell. I had to learn to get out of my own way on this. I was in the way of letting my practice become a business that was not dependent on me. I thought in my mind I needed to be involved. I thought good leadership meant rolling up my sleeves and showing others how it was done. In reality, I was creating a practice in which I was the main value proposition. While this might be a profitable way of doing business, it is challenging to sell. Most practitioners are not taught this distinction. On the contrary, our formal training teaches us to be the doer. We are the clinicians. We are the experts. You don't get awards for collaboration or leadership in dental school. With some urging from people like Dan Kennedy, I became clear about becoming **the business owner, not the producer**. I was determined to do it right when I rebuilt my practice. I built a team and the systems needed to remove myself from the operations. I brought in multiple associate doctors to become the producers. I focused on leadership, culture, and systems. In short, I built a real business instead of a practice where I was the center. This is a key aspect of selling your practice *for top dollar*.

DAN: This is not as hard as it may sound. Most of the obstacles are in the owner's mind, not in reality. Even I had to do this with my main business when it was sold. It was a personality-based business with me at its center and active in every income stream. I reduced, then took myself out of one income production activity and deliverable after another, transitioning to others leading some of our mastermind groups, others doing coaching, certain vendors taking over services sold to members, and, in my mind, moving from the *Superman* comic book to the *Justice League of America*. Bill, my first buyer, and I, continuing with active roles, worked on this over several years to ultimately position the company for sale. Just as it did in your case, it took us about 3 years to make all the changes.

What other lessons did you learn, with your boomerang experience?

DR. PHELPS: Your practice is only as strong as your financials: Accounting is often considered an afterthought. It is done after the fact for tax purposes. Most practices have a bookkeeper and a CPA who files taxes once per year. When selling your practice, your practice is only as valuable as your financials. Your practice should have the financial dashboards and KPIs in place that allow you to make actionable decisions based on real-time information. Most practitioners do not realize how much their practice is leaking money simply because they do not have data to provide a clear picture of leading and lagging indicators in their business.

DAN: It's interesting that you say that. I talk to business owners all the time who get all their financial information in ill-usable form, too late to make use of. In my book—forgive the plug— *No B.S. Ruthless Management of People and Profits*, there is a whole chapter on what I call "money math," the numbers that matter to you, not your CPA or the IRS. I'd also make the point that when a potential buyer looks at your normal numbers on normal P/Ls, if you can show them numbers they didn't even know to ask about, that you monitor hourly, daily, or weekly, and use for something more than recordkeeping, you can alter the entire conversation. So, I'm going to dare to restate something you said: Your business is only as valuable as your financials *and the way you present them.*

Last tip, from your experience…

DR. PHELPS: Take time and mount a search to find the right guides and advisors. The first time I sold my practice, I thought I could figure it out on my own. Sure, I was a good clinician and an expert in my field of practice. I even had extensive deal-making experience in real estate, but I had never sold a business before. I was in uncharted territory, and I made costly mistakes. Just because you've been highly successful running your business does not automatically guarantee you'll be highly successful at selling it. Michael Jordan spent a year trying to play pro baseball.

DAN: Now, in your current business, you are predominately spending time advising dentists on their post-sale finances and lives. There's a whole chapter on this coming up, Chapter 16, with Ted Oakley, but I'd like you to go ahead and weigh in on it. I've sold my practice—now what?

DR. PHELPS: Often, the real limitation that keeps practitioners from selling their practice or that causes them to sabotage the process before successfully selling is not the mechanics of the sale itself, but rather questions of what comes after. How much money is enough? What is my financial plan post-practice sale? What's my next?? What will I do or who will I be when I no longer have my practice? Without a clear plan, the uncertainty surrounding these questions can keep practitioners trapped and fearful from venturing into the unknown.

What I realized relatively early in my life, due to my moment of truth brought on by my daughter's health crisis, is that the big question to be faced when selling your practice is: "How much is enough?" Most people never know, and that question keeps them on the treadmill—grinding it out much longer than they really need to. If you're running on that treadmill because you don't know how much is enough, and you want to be a good financial provider for your family, I get that. You never know how much is enough, so you just keep doing more and more. More practices and a bigger office, and piling up more money in the 401(k). There is never an end to that. That uncertainty will linger with you forever until you first learn how to make your money work for you sustainably and predictably. And that's not going to happen in the stock market.

View a practice sale not just as a business transaction, but as a significant investment decision. Historically, professionals like doctors and engineers have been taught to prioritize technical or clinical expertise over financial acumen. The result is that many transition from practitioner to investor without the skill sets and experience needed to thrive. A practice sale is not only a business transaction, it is an investment move—shifting capital from one asset, your practice, into another. What is your plan? Into what assets do you plan to deploy your capital for maximum security and predictable returns? If you get this right, you may realize you can sell and exit sooner than you thought possible, walking away with less now than more much later.

DAN: OK, how do you get this right? How can you safely leave earlier with less rather than waiting and waiting and waiting to hopefully get more?

DR. PHELPS: The key to financial stability post-exit lies in having a well-developed plan to create replacement income through investing while shielding your capital from volatility, market corrections, and inflation. Historical trends, like the 2008 financial crisis, have shown that relying solely on traditional financial markets like stocks and bonds sold to you by Wall Street for this income can be risky, especially in the face of inflation and market volatility.

Beware of risking and exposing your hard-earned proceeds from the sale of your practice to the volatility of the markets. Emphasis should be placed on replacement income streams from investments that can be relied on to replace active income generation. The goal is to secure your financial future without returning to trading time for income. This is the essence of my Freedom Founders philosophy—which begins with reaching one's freedom number via investment cash flow vs. being dependent on your active income. I and members of my Freedom Founders group principally use income-generating real estate for this purpose— *without* chasing deals, taking on risky debt, being a contractor or repairman or landlord. Over the last 12 years, I have helped guide hundreds of practice owners through transitioning from practice owner to their "next." It began organically as colleagues privately asked me to confide the pathway I took to selling my practice and achieving financial security in my early 40s.

One such colleague, Dr. Dennis Perry, an oral surgeon from Ohio, initially tried to sell his practice and retire on his 401(k) a few years before we met. His financial advisors told him that he would have enough assets to last until he was 92—"as long as we don't see a major correction in the markets in the first few years of your retirement." What kind of assurance is that?? Is that lack of certainty what you've worked 35–40 years to create? Their plan called for a steady drawdown of principal over the course of his remaining years until the nest egg ran dry at age 92. But what if he lives longer than 92? What if he faced a wholly unexpected, big expense? This "plan" is really no plan at all. But it's the best that Wall Street has to offer.

Fast-forward to today. Dennis has transitioned his investments off Wall Street and into income-producing real estate assets. He is living entirely off of the income that his investments are producing. He isn't spending a dollar of his principal. In fact, his nest egg is growing in retirement. Not only is this approach

100 percent sustainable, it will create a significant legacy to pass on to his children and grandchildren.

DAN: I want to give you an opportunity to describe your Freedom Founders associate and how it works.

DR. PHELPS: You need a place where truth, wisdom, *and experience* are present. You need deep connections in a network of like-minded people who share your values. No one has a crystal ball. We can't predict exactly when/where these changes will take place. But whatever happens, it must not be faced alone. After a long journey with a lot of ups and downs, today I have the privilege of being surrounded by and leading a tribe of smart, seasoned, freedom-loving professionals who share my core values and believe in what I believe. A tribe of individuals committed to preserving and expanding wealth, creating replacement income, and exiting their practices in 3 to 7 years. We support each other with information, experience, and use of a well-proven blueprint.

DR. DAVID PHELPS, DDS, created the Freedom Founders community in 2012 to help dentists and other professionals take control of their retirement investments to produce passive cash flow, security, peace of mind, and the freedom to live life on their terms. To contact Dr. Phelps, visit www.FreedomFounders.com.

CHAPTER 14

Interview with Stan Kinder

What Dentists Must Know to Maximize Value When Selling and All Business Owners Need to Translate and Consider

DAN: Stan Kinder is a specialist, as an advisor and as a broker, in the sale and purchase of dental practices. However, it was clear in my reading of Stan's work that he belonged in this book. He is concise and clear. While he speaks "dental practice," every business owner can learn from and translate him.

Stan, let's start with why dentists make mistakes—costly mistakes—when selling.

STAN: Most dentists will only sell a practice once during their professional career—typically as they approach retirement. So, it comes as no surprise they are naïve and uninformed about the ins and outs of how to achieve the best value.

DAN: I don't think business owners give this enough thought—that, for most, this is a financial event that is only going to occur once in their entire lives. Most people buy three, four, five houses during their lives. They try to marry just once, but about half do that two or more times. Many start a 401(k), contribute to it, and don't pay much attention to it. But the most permanent, irreversible thing most business owners do is sell and exit. I also don't think they give themselves enough room to be careful and to get help. What you said is brilliant: It should come as no surprise you're not smart about this since you've never done it before. Were you good enough after your first game of poker to pony up entry fees and play in tournaments? When Warren Buffett got interested in bridge, he hired a tutor. When Arnold Palmer needed to change his golf swing late in his career because of age, when Peyton Manning had to reengineer his throwing motion, they got coaches. I imagine you've seen every mistake. What are the most common?

STAN: The most common value-crushing mistake practice sellers make is waiting to sell their practice when it is in decline. Most dental practices follow a predictable life cycle—early years of consistent and steady growth, followed by years of plateaued performance mid-career, and ending in steady decline as the owner dentist decreases his or her psychological, emotional, and time commitment to the practice. Far too many dentists choose to sell their practice when it is in this end stage, at a lower value and for far less money than would otherwise be the case. So, the first and most important lesson is to be thoughtful and deliberate about planning your practice transition and exit strategy. This is the path that will enable you to achieve maximum value consistent with your financial, retirement, and life goals.

DAN: There's nothing you just said that wouldn't apply to almost any small company with its founder at its helm. How can an owner figure out when he should sell the company? Or, what other questions should he answer?

STAN: Here are six big questions I like to discuss with the would-be seller:
1. Why am I selling? Examples might include retirement, bringing in a growth partner, or diminishing the administrative burden, among any number of others.
2. How does the sale of my practice integrate with my overall retirement planning?
3. Do I want to continue working after the sale or do I prefer to sell and walk away?
4. Would I consider working longer if I could unload the burdens of practice ownership?
5. What is my target financial outcome, and more broadly, what is vitally important to me as I pursue a sale?
6. What is my ideal timeline?

Answering these questions will help you focus on the why, when, how, and who of your desired transition. This leads to the next consideration—how to obtain maximum value at the time of sale.

The first, and most important, thing to understand is that the central foundation of value in selling your practice is free cash flow, the dollars on your bottom line. It is not your state-of-the-art facility, your wonderful staff, or even your loyal patients. In the final analysis, these variables are important only to the degree that they help or hinder the production of net income. There is a principle at the core of every approach to valuing a practice, and it is this—**the primary driver of practice value is the cash flow generated by the practice that will be available to the purchaser to pay himself a living income and to support the cost of the purchase.** Consequently, net income is the basis for the purest measure of practice value. This is true not only for the dentist buyer, but it is also true for a DSO buyer seeking a return on the capital they invest to acquire a practice.

The implication of this is pretty clear. If you want more value when you sell, you need to think creatively and aggressively about how to create more profit in your practice.

DAN: One of my books in this No B.S. series is *No B.S. Ruthless Management of People and Profits*. Key words: "and profits." You may be able to raise your selling price by special features or aspects of your business, by synergy with a buyer, by other methods laid out throughout this book. But you can't put icing on a bad cake and sell it for a top price, can you? When we were preparing the Inner Circle business, then GKIC, standing for Glazer-Kennedy Inner Circle, we spent a year rearranging a number of things in the business to improve profits, even at the expense of growth. We stopped a few frills, which erased some expenses and boosted profits. Candidly, over time, this would have been a mistake, but in the short term its negative effects didn't show themselves, and increased profits did.

STAN: That's right. Smart business owners go through a very thorough process of bolstering profits leading up to taking a company to market. One of the easiest and most accessible ways to do this in the practice is to increase the number of high-fee elective procedures you perform—such as implants. This falls into the bucket of "working smarter, not harder" approaches. There are proven marketing models available to achieve the desired outcome. A great example is the "Sell More Implants" and "Ultimate Marketing Machine" programs available from Parthiv Shah and his firm eLaunchers. You can learn more at SellMoreImplants.com. His program is effective both for practitioners who place and restore implants and those who only restore, referring the placement out to a specialist.

Here's an important note on this issue of creating additional profits. Depending on who the buyer is, each additional dollar of profit can potentially result in $5, $6, or even more in increased purchase price, creating a "multiplier" effect.

A corollary consideration related to the profit question is the quality of your financial records. Every buyer will use these records to calculate your profit, and it is imperative that they are clear, accurate, and understandable. Any inconsistencies will sow doubt in the mind of the buyer—which inevitably leads to a lower valuation or no deal at all.

Another pathway to improved profits is by implementing more efficient operating systems and better expense control. The fastest way to achieve this is with the help of a coach/consultant. There are many proven performers available to you. Some of the leading examples include Dr. John Meis, Fortune Management, MGE Consultants, and Renegade Millionaire® Mastermind. Any of these would be great candidates to help you raise and accelerate your practice's performance.

DAN: If I may, I'll add two more to the list to look at: Jay Geier, Scheduling Institute, and Dr. Emily Letran, DrEmilyLetran. com. I'll also plug another of my books: *Almost Alchemy: More from Fewer and Less*. It includes my Found Money Map to do just that: find money hidden inside your business. I think the owner needs to make a project of this. Gather information. Study up. Investigate different consultants and coaches. Obviously, they can come and talk to you. Make sure they have the right CPA for this job. Next, let's talk about getting paid.

STAN: Who the buyer is matters greatly. There are profound differences in how two types of buyers value practices. These differences can result in hundreds of thousands and, in some cases, millions of dollars more being paid to the practice seller. Let me explain.

When you sell your practice to a dentist, unless you are willing to hold the paper, and finance the sale yourself, the dentist buyer is relying on a bank loan for the purchase. In this situation, the big variable is how much a bank is willing to lend. Historically, banks have capped their loan limits at 60–80 percent of top-line revenue, independent of all other considerations. In some rare cases, they would loan 100 percent, but this rarely happens in today's higher interest rate environment. The dentist buyer's primary concerns at the time of purchase are: How much can I pay myself? And how will I be able to repay the loan? The latter is also the bank's primary concern—is there sufficient cash flow to enable predictable loan repayment?

On the other hand, the DSO buyer is making an allocation of capital investment decision and is focused on ROI—return on investment. There are three drivers that often enable the DSO to pay much higher values.

1. They do not have the same dependency on bank debt to finance the purchase. Most DSOs are private equity funded and have ready access to capital.

2. They benefit from the arbitrage opportunity in the difference in value for a single stand-alone practice and the much higher value of a practice as a constituent member in a large integrated network.

3. Their confidence in their ability to bring economies of scale to reduce expenses and their operating and capital capabilities to grow revenue and profits.

Let's examine how this difference played out in a real transaction. The practice in question is a single-site practice located in the central mid-Atlantic with revenues of $2,374,003 in the 12 months preceding the sale. I'll tell you the price actually paid by a DSO, and the expected price in a traditional bank-financed sale to a dentist. With the DSO buyer, the sale closed with $7,275,000 in value being paid to the owner dentist. For the sake of making a strong comparison, let's assume the dentist buyer was able to secure a loan at 100 percent of revenue, $2,374,003. Admittedly, the profit margin in this practice was well above average, but we're still talking a difference of nearly $5 million to the seller. Going back to the "multiplier effect" mentioned earlier—in the DSO option, each incremental dollar of profit would result in an increase of a little over $7 in increased purchase price and no increase at all in the dentist buyer option. Even if that dentist buyer was adding capital of his own to the bank's loan, and he was willing to pay a premium for certain reasons, that sale might, at the very best, be about $4 million. This "multiplier effect" makes it a no-brainer to spend money to improve your procedure mix, or to get help improving your performance. Let me say that again: It's a no-brainer to SPEND MONEY on improving profits.

You can easily see that who the buyer is matters greatly. Having said that, a DSO transaction is not for everybody, and not every practice will be attractive to a DSO buyer. The vast majority of DSOs require the seller to commit to a 6-year employment agreement post-transaction. If your goal is to sell and walk away, then a DSO buyer is not for you, no matter the financial differences.

DAN: To generalize, this same dynamic exists in most other types of businesses. Who the buyer is and how they are going to pay for the purchase, what they *can* put together for the purchase, matters.

Some version of the PE-funded DSO now exists in a number of business categories. In many, not with the dental practice, there is the upstream corporate buyer. Chapter 3 talks about different buyers. You can figure out what type of buyer is most likely to satisfy you with the best mix of price, terms, post-sale arrangements, and make sure the business is "dressed up" to appeal to those buyers. Stan, thanks; this has been fantastic information.

If you would like advice or assistance with a sale,
whether to a DSO or a dentist, simply send an email to
stan@everythingdso.com and he will help in any way he can.

CHAPTER 15

Interview with Jonathan Cronstedt
Adventures of "The $2 Billion Man"

DAN: Jonathan Cronstedt grew a tech company by 2,153 percent in 5 years, to a $2 billion valuation. He describes it as a grand *adventure*. He now helps other entrepreneurs, principally in tech and software and AI spaces, grow start-ups or existing companies in ways that get them ready for sale at top dollar. Jonathan, let's talk about lessons learned while on your adventure…

JC: My first dealings with private equity and institutional investors taught me a lot about structure. Most entrepreneurs get fixated on The Number—the exit valuation and selling price they want—and they scale up to justify that, and they're very excited when they hit it. But let's say your number is a $10 million exit, and I offer you the $10 million you ask for—did you get your goal? Maybe. Maybe not. I might offer you $2 million in cash at closing, a note you hold for $6 million dependent on future performance, and an additional $2 million earn-out tied to your working and helping the company hit certain goals. That's structure.

DAN: David Melrose can speak from experience about the performance-based note, and about tiny little poison pills that can be in it, to make ever collecting on it a challenge even if the buyer competently ruins the business, which often does not occur. The individual who bought my company, then later sold it, experienced the trickiness of earn-out money. You are right on target about this.

JC: Well, in my example, you actually got only 20 percent of your goal number, with 80 percent to be collected in the future, but that might not be collected.

DAN: You can tell your golfing buddies you got a $10-million-dollar deal, and that's true, but it's *not* $10 million. The same realities apply when bringing investors and partners in, selling parts of or shares in the company, right?

JC: At our company, Kajabi, we were very fortunate. We had incredibly supportive equity partners that, at every juncture, if we were splitting a nickel, they gave us three pennies. But I've seen too many entrepreneurs subject to an entirely different fate, having ignored structure in their eagerness to get a deal, to get a round of capital raising done.

DAN: What's next, in a complicated sale?

JC: The LOI, the Letter of Intent. Most entrepreneurs see that as if it was a check. It has their number on it, but subject to revision. So, growth and profit while building is obviously important; what happens to the company's performance after the LOI, between the LOI and actual closing, is *extremely* important. What often happens, that we didn't let happen, is the team disengages, key people leave or are circulating resumes, your own focus shifts, and the ether of liquidity overshadows the things that got you to the LOI. Performance slips. Numbers weaken. And your valuation gets reduced. This is a time of asymmetrical downside. A 5 percent or 10 percent variation in revenue or growth or profit or other metric isn't alarming to you. It's just business. But for your buyer, they've now been armed with a weapon to allege concern, to question some systemic problem represented by the fluctuation. It is all about multiples. Whether a big part of your selling price is a multiple of revenue or a multiple of EBITDA, it's still a multiple. That 5 percent or 10 percent forecast miss, if just $100,000, could trigger a reduction of enterprise value of $500,000 to $2 million.

DAN: How do you manage this?

JC: You have to keep it a sprint. During the due diligence after the LOI, you'll be asked more questions and asked for more documents than you ever thought possible. Dan, what you call Deal-Killers may even be deliberately slowing things down. If they're paid by the hour, perverse incentive. The LOI is the start, not the finish line. Revenue or profit hiccups have a multiplied effect. Time is not your friend. You have to keep sprinting and push and pull your buyer and its team with you. At the same time, you have to stay focused on the company's performance.

You also have to be alert for unscrupulous buyers. They'll put a big number on an LOI they never intend to pay, to get your business off the market and lock you in to exclusivity and then "pencil whip" you, using every number, every fluctuation, the slightest inconsistency found to beat you down to a much lower valuation or different terms. They hope you'll be so exhausted with the process that you'll just want it to be over, and accept a much lower number than you would otherwise. If you're playing in the big leagues, with investment bankers, considering competing LOIs, ask about the track record of closings of each one of them. The LOI with the best numbers may not be the best at all.

DAN: I recall each time the company I created was sold, a time of sweating bullets between the LOI and the closing. For a small company, that period of time was very disruptive. The worst one was the sale to PE. The others, to companies run by great entrepreneurs, were easier. One observation I have about the due diligence is that, often, they ask for things that don't matter and overlook really important things. Let's shift, to growth. How much growth? Is revenue growth a trap or a necessity? When do we look at profit?

JC: There has been a period of time, fueled by low interest rates and enormous liquidity, when fortunes were made on the philosophy that all growth is good growth, and as long as you're growing fast enough, profitability doesn't matter.

A lot of companies were basically selling $100 bills for $20, as long as somebody would finance it. An example is Bolt Commerce, once worth $11 billion; now, as we talk, worth 3 percent of that. When interest rates jumped up, other macro problems reared up, this changed. But it was never healthy. Sure, if you time it right, you may exit the burning building before it collapses with a big bag of money, but also with a badly damaged reputation. Even though we were tech, we always believed profit mattered. Kajabi was a bootstrapped company that was always profitable. This allowed us to stay true to our purpose, choose financial partners more carefully, and have a self-sustainable business. When you are profitable, you can sell because you want to, when you want to, not trying to time the market or, worse, selling because you have to, because of the market.

DAN: I talk about this as fake growth with fake money versus real growth with real money. But people are going to be asking how you could grow as big and fast as you did AND be profitable. Most believe you must sacrifice profit to growth.

JC: We have to get into your areas of expertise. With clients and others, I'm sharing what we did with…I talk a lot about pricing, margins, and a lot of entrepreneurs underprice to try and buy growth. You need really effective advertising and marketing, and insist that it and the media you use produces, or you stop it. Or you need the Product to be so contagious that the importance of advertising is reduced. In 5 years, we achieved 2,153 percent growth. In 2015, Kajabi was at $6 million in sales. Five years later, over $100 million and a $2 billion valuation. From that, I developed what I teach and consult on, my 7-Step Billion Dollar Bulls-Eye Formula. Here's why it's important: At least half of the wealth you will ever amass from your business will come on the day you sell it. So, scaling your business to its maximum potential value is more important than anything else you might accomplish with that business.

DAN: Do you want to just give an overview of the formula?

JC: You have to be incredibly smart or get help from incredibly smart people to absolutely excel in these 7 Ps:
- Purpose
- Profit
- Product
- Prestige
- Promotion
- Persuasion
- People

If somebody wants a more complete dive into this, they can get it at JCRON.com. A key point is that these ducks have to be put in a row in the order I listed them.

DAN: I want to divert just briefly to, as you said, where I live most, marketing. You did a very smart and patient thing at the very beginning.

JC: This was all my partner, Kenny Rueter. He spent over a year coding before Kajabi ever went live. But at the same time—

DAN: In my Renegade Millionaire System®, I call this *simultaneous, not sequential.*

JC: That's right. At the same time, he built a wait-list for the product by doing free work with a mini-Kajabi for select industry leaders. He called it *marketing to the front row.* That let Kajabi start with over $1 million ARR instantly at launch.

DAN: Okay, let's loop back. We know most businesses taken to market, put up for sale, do not sell. Of those that do, half do so for considerably less money or on poorer terms than the owners wanted. Why all this disappointment and failure?

JC: One, size. Institutional buyers, and what you call upstream buyers, want to buy big, not small. If you're too small, you rule out an entire category of potential buyers. Two is probably the perceived fragility of the company because of the key people hazard.

DAN: Let's talk about that. About you and the key man issue, and about the levers of power that built your company's value.

JC: Even though we all know systems are important, we tend to fall into The Key Man Trap. Or: Key Woman. I'll bet as somebody is reading this, the images of their key man, their key woman pop right to mind. Probably starting with them. You can immediately think of that person or those people that, without them, all would be lost. Some entrepreneurs actually have no interest in systems. They rely on people doing things right, getting things done. They have people they have a lot of confidence in. But an acquirer will not share that confidence. When it is realized that the business is dependent on certain key people, you've got problems with its sale. Even if your buyer is in your industry, has know-how and experience, even has staff to step in if needed, you have still handed them a weapon for negotiation.

DAN: In another chapter, Dr. Phelps talks about this with his dental practice—making it function independent of him. We faced it with a business driven by two people as personalities—as tribe leaders—so, to his credit, the man I sold to and then worked with for years systemized most of the other aspects of the company, especially on the recurring revenue side. The utopia, though, is 100 percent systems run, isn't it?

JC: Warren Buffett said that he tries to invest in businesses that are so wonderful an idiot can run them—because sooner or later, one will. This is not so much about the type of business Warren will buy or invest in. That is a variety. It's about how much the business is run by systems and how much by people. That doesn't mean some buyers won't buy a company to really buy its talent. But for the majority of businesses sold and bought, the key person trap gets in the way; the systems thing helps a lot.

DAN: Next reason deals don't happen?

JC: Bad numbers. I say: No numbers, no business. Know numbers know business. But which numbers matter? I've divided these into three levels of numbers. NOTE: SEE LIST, END OF THIS CHAPTER, PAGE 131

DAN: There is a lot we could talk about in each of your Ps. Your story of turning off $1 million of ad spend with no harm done is chilling and instructive. Unfortunately, we have only so much time for this, only so many pages of the book. Do you have an ending thought?

JC: There are a lot of fundamentally good businesses that never get sold, potentially good deals that never get made, mostly because entrepreneurs don't put enough into scaling, preparing, and presenting the business. They may be too casual about it. They may just delegate it to a broker or investment bank. We were convinced from the start that our successful valuation would be because of what WE did.

JONATHAN CRONSTEDT is an author, speaker, advisor, and investor, the former President, now Board Director of Kajabi. You can reach Jonathan at JCRON.com.

The Numbers You Need
to Track & Present to Buyers

Level One
- Revenue
- Gross Profit Margin
- Net Profit Margin
- Cash Flow
- Return on Investment

Level Two
- Accounts Receivable/Collections/Cash Turnover
- Inventory Turnover
- Debt to Equity Ratio
- Customer Acquisition Cost
- Lifetime Customer Value

Level Three
- Customer Retention Rate
- Lead to Close Ratio
- Employee Turnover Rate
- Profit per Customer

CHAPTER 16

Interview with Ted Oakley

NOW WHAT?
$10 Million, $30 Million, $50 Million, AND BROKE!

DAN: Ted Oakley, founder and CEO of Oxbow Advisors, provides wealth management and related services to individuals and families who have recently sold, are selling, or are getting ready to sell their companies. He manages money for me and for my co-author, David Melrose. Ted is the author of a number of books, including *The Psychology of Staying Rich,* and is a frequent guest on investment-oriented podcasts and TV programs including *Opening Bell with Maria Bartiromo* on FOX Business.

Ted, one of your books is titled *CRAZY TIME,* about surviving the first 12 months after selling your company. You note that surveys of sellers of companies have over 75 percent say they were *unhappy* within a year after the sale. This is really an astounding statistic. After all, selling your company and walking away from it—the stress and responsibilities with tens of millions of dollars—is supposed to make you happy. Why doesn't it? And why is that so dangerous?

TED: Many business owners have their entire life and sense of worth tied up in their business. In other words, ego. Everybody is calling them "boss"—they are the #1 player on the field. It's like what happens with many pro athletes—when they leave the field permanently, everything stops.

DAN: It's actually a much bigger and dramatic change than most people expect. It sort of puts everything that's left in a new spotlight, doesn't it?

TED: For example, how happy are you with your marriage? Now you'll be spending a lot more time with your spouse. Next, can you change your purpose from just making money in business? All this is dangerous because, when it happens, days or weeks after the sale, it's a shock and it creates a vacuum. There's danger in: What will I fill this vacuum with?

DAN: Quoting you again, you've said that "all the skills and instincts that served the business owner well as an entrepreneur fail him in that first year or so, in his new freedom as an investor and caretaker of his money." In your book *$20 MILLION AND BROKE*, you say: You may be an entrepreneur with a lot of money, but that does *not* make you a good investor. Entrepreneurs, myself included, have strong egos. I know from my clients who've sold that there *is* the assumption that what got them there will continue to make them successful going forward—why is that such a bad assumption?

TED: Selling a company for a lot of money makes you FEEL very successful, which you are. What it does not tell you is that, while you've been very successful in your business, that doesn't mean you have any knowledge or skills about any other business. I see some people sell for a lot of money, rush to open what's called a "family office," and start doing deals. Most go badly, because the person does not know enough about the businesses he is investing in. He's not ready to run them. Because of ego swelled up by the sale, it's very hard to hear or tell yourself: "I'm not capable of that." I use Charlie Munger's quote: "Knowing what you don't know is more useful than being brilliant."

DAN: I think *some* skills are universally transferable, but each different situation also requires new, specific knowledge and, as the cliché says, the devil is in the details. In another book of yours, *DANGER TIME: THE TWO-YEAR RED ZONE AFTER SELLING YOUR COMPANY,* you lay out three steps or phases. #1 is: Slow Down. #2: Fund Your Life. #3: Stick to Basics. Would you talk about those?

TED: The slow-down phase should go something like this: If you can, take your assistant from your company with you. That person has probably been working with you for 10 or 20 years or longer, knows you better than most people. Set up an office somewhere. Get organized. A good thing about this is that you'll feel productive, but your pace will be slowed. Second, fund your life. You have to figure out how much money, after taxes, you are going to need to spend. A supply of money set aside, safe, just for that has to be established before you do anything else. I recommend waiting a year before doing any new business deals or anything but basic investing. Remember, before, when somebody at a cocktail party bragged about making a killing with something you weren't familiar with, your money was locked up in your business, preventing you from doing anything crazy. Now it's not.

DAN: When I referred David Melrose to you, after his sale, you convinced him to lock up most of the money in the most conservative of investments and do nothing with it for 12 months. You kept him out of the market. He has told me on more than one occasion that he had impulses this stopped, and that he is very glad he followed your advice. He thinks it saved millions. "Do nothing" is so antithetical to an entrepreneur, this is really uncomfortable. But it's such good advice because entrepreneurs *underestimate the drama* of the changes that selling a company creates. First, the seller has a big bucket of cash. He may NEVER have had that before. His wealth was inside his company—now it is let loose, all at once. I have a favorite old, bad joke about this. Guy walks into a bar with a big, shaggy mutt, and they sit side by side on barstools. Guy orders two beers. The bartender says, "You can't bring a dog in here." Guy says, "Look, it's the middle of the afternoon. There's nobody here. And the dog can do a trick you just won't believe if you want to see it." Bartender gives in. Guy puts a $5 bill in the dog's mouth and tells it to go fetch him a pack of smokes. Dog's back lickety-split with a pack of Marlboros. Bartender is properly amazed and wants to try it. He pulls a $20 bill out of his pocket, puts it in the dog's mouth, and tells him to fetch another pack of cigarettes. Ten minutes later, no dog. Twenty minutes, no dog. They go looking for him. Dog's out in the alley, to say it politely, having crazed doggie-style sex with a little white poodle. His owner screams at him and yells, "What are you doing?" Dog says, "Hey, I never had twenty bucks *before.*"

Second, his income stops. The paycheck or direct deposit to his personal account on the 1st and 15th that he and his spouse are used to disappears. Three, perks go away, too. The company was paying for the car lease, some vacation trips tied to business conferences. Fourth, people think of them as lottery winners and descend on them with needs, requests for money, and business ideas. There's a lot. There's also their surprise at how they are treated by the buyer after the sale. Can you talk a little more about how sellers you've worked with cope with all this successfully— and how others fail at it?

TED: The people that sell their business and do well at it understand *completely* that they sold, somebody else bought, and life has changed. They understand that the way they were a Big Deal is past, and they are a Nobody in that world. The ones who are bitterly disappointed and frustrated—and made desperate to replace their power—had the idea that the new owners are going to listen to them, seek advice from them, treat them as very important. Nine out of 10 times that doesn't happen. I can't give you one case where 3 years down the road, the buyer is still listening to the seller. The people who sell and do well also understand that there are more, maybe bigger changes going on in their lives. The seller's routine changed, but the spouse's didn't. Suddenly expecting that, to be the center of the spouse's attention, is a recipe for disaster. Same with the adult kids. They have to find replacements for everything they were getting intellectually and emotionally from running their business without putting their new, finite wealth at undue risk doing it. This is one of the places I come in, helping the individual client develop a new plan. It's not just—choose me to hand your wealth over to, to manage. It's also—how are you going to manage *you*, and how can I help.

DAN: Let's talk about the bucket of money itself. Give me your top five pieces of advice about me suddenly having what feels like a huge fortune certain to last forever…

TED: First, wait until having the big money feels normal. What I've seen in working with sellers of companies over the years is that when they first get that big check, it feels surreal to them. It takes a little while to be calm and rational about it. Any impulse to immediately run out and buy a boat should be resisted.

Second, try your best to put most or all of this money into bulletproof investments while you think about things. People will come—from Wall Street, from local banks, with business deals that you don't know anything about. Family will have needs. You'll think, "Well, this is only $500,000 and we have $20 million. We can afford it." Before you know it, you'll have $18 million.

Third, as I said before, busy yourself setting up a small, simple office. Take your assistant with you or at least hire a part-time assistant. This will make the transition easier.

Fourth, you need to become the greatest listener in the world. Carefully. When you talk with people in real estate, private business, investments, you need to just listen. Gather information. Let yourself be intrigued. Try to remember how observant and curious you were when you first started out in the business you just sold.

Fifth, enjoy and set out to enjoy the success you've created. You are here for less than 100 years. You've used up quite a few. You don't have anything to prove. And if you are thinking about your children and grandchildren a lot, a good project is writing down your story so that they know how your wealth was made and what it took to make it. By the way, you can get a copy of my own short book, *My Story*, at Amazon or at OxbowAdvisors.com.

DAN: I'm staying on money. We'll loop back to family. You've said that Wall Street is ultimately all about selling, and the hype is endless. I see one FOMO event after another promoted. You say, quote: "Don't be *afraid* to be conservative." The word "afraid" jumped out at me. Why would people feel this way? How does Wall Street leverage this?

TED: People are actually afraid to be conservative investors, or ashamed of it. They go to a cocktail party and they hear the stories of brilliant moves and huge gains. Dan Kennedy drove professionally in harness races for 20 years, as a vocation, not an occupation. In his office, walls are covered with Win photos. I was there when somebody said, "Wow! You won all those races?" He said, "We don't put the photos from the races I lost up on the wall." Same with these cocktail-party, country-club, Thanksgiving-dinner win stories. You watch business news on TV and see reports of people making huge gains in this or that. You start to think, "Maybe I'm in the wrong spot." You are ashamed to be the one without a big story—as if having built a successful company and sold it wasn't enough. There's a lot of pressure to take *unnecessary* risks.

DAN: I'll give you a little chance here to describe your philosophy of investing and managing people's wealth at Oxbow Advisors...

TED: When we manage money for clients at Oxbow, we stand for and stand against certain things. For example, we'll fight you on large drawdowns of wealth. It takes too long to make it up, and the mental effects are more than most people can handle. We are for preservation of capital. Our main approach is to separate the money into Base Capital and Investment Capital. Base Capital has to be there, permanently, always. This prevents you from being scared to death or irrationally impulsive when others are. Only the designated Investment Capital gets invested, and it gets further separated. Third, we want you to be happy and for your spouse to be happy. If you spend your time trying to beat the S&P for the rest of your life, you are going to be a sad, anxious, frustrated human being. There are more achievable goals, like creating a return above the inflation rate, so your buying power stays the same over 5, 15, 25 years. Our clients want to stay rich, not try getting giant gains or get a lot richer at the cost of giant uncertainty. We politely turn away about two out of every five new clients who come to us, when we find their values and objectives in conflict with ours and our investment models.

DAN: I'm going to end in a difficult space: about family. In *$20 MILLION AND BROKE*, you say that some wise parents are able to help their children recognize their privileged status, respect it, and make it on their own. Many parents are worried about this, frustrated by it, and are unable to convey their values. This is tough to hear and tough to admit. I'll admit it's a struggle for me, with kids and grandkids and siblings. I've seen it a much, much bigger problem for some of my clients. So people don't feel alone in this—how big of an issue do you find it to be? And what are some cautions you have about dealing with money and family?

TED: When people come into a lot of money, by selling their company or some other liquidity event, they often start thinking about making sure life is *easier* for their children and grandchildren than it was for them, or giving them complete financial security. This is bad financial strategy and, frankly, bad parenting. They must know how money is earned, made, saved, and know how to stand on their own two feet, and know they know it. It should be "tough" for a period of time. Bringing them into the family office at age 21 and giving them authority they haven't earned and responsibility they haven't prepared for is a big mistake. I find this is a big concern for my clients. Tactically or technically, there are, of course, investment, estate plan, and other ways to exercise control over family wealth over generations, and those options should be considered. But the biggest question is: What do you really want to accomplish with your children and grandchildren? It's probably *not* just making them rich with your money!

TED OAKLEY is an author, speaker, and media guest expert
and the CEO of the specialized wealth management firm
Oxbow Advisors serving clients throughout the U.S. and Canada.
His books are available at Amazon and at OxbowAdvisors.com,
along with a number of videos and other resources.

Other Books
by the Author

Other Books in The NO B.S. Series

No B.S. Guide to Marketing Automation with Parthiv Shah (2024)

No B.S. Time Management for Entrepreneurs, Fourth Edition with Ben Glass (2024)

No B.S. Direct Marketing, Fourth Edition with Darcy Juarez and Marty Fort (2024)

No B.S. How to Succeed in Business by Breaking All the Rules (2024)

The Best of No B.S. (2022)

No B.S. Guide to Direct Response Social Media Marketing, Second Edition, with Kim Walsh Phillips, (2020)

No B.S. Marketing to the Affluent, Third Edition (2019)

No B.S. Time Management for Entrepreneurs, Third Edition (2017)

No B.S. Guide to Powerful Presentations
   with Dustin Mathews (2017)

No B.S. Guide to Maximum Referrals and Customer Retention
   with Shaun Buck (2016)

No B.S. Ruthless Management of People and Profits,
   Second Edition (2014)

No B.S. Guide to Brand-Building by Direct Response (2014)

No B.S. Trust Based Marketing with Matt Zagula (2012)

No B.S. Grassroots Marketing with Jeff Slutsky (2012)

No B.S. Guide to Marketing to Leading Edge Boomers & Seniors
   with Chip Kessler (2012)

No B.S. Price Strategy with Jason Marrs (2011)

No B.S. Business Success in the New Economy (2010)

No B.S. Sales Success in the New Economy (2010)

No B.S. Wealth Attraction in the New Economy (2010)

Forthcoming NO B.S. Books

No B.S. Marketing to the Affluent, Fourth Edition
   with Martin Fischer (2025)

Other Books of Note by Dan S. Kennedy

Almost Alchemy: Make Any Business of Any Size Produce More with Fewer and Less (Forbes Books, 2019)

My Unfinished Business: Autobiographical Essays (Advantage, 2009)

The New Psycho-Cybernetics with Dr. Maxwell Maltz (Prentice-Hall Press, 2002)

AUDIO BOOKS are available at Audible.com.

Index